LIFE'S ABIDING RESOURCES

To
Azora
My Gracious Lady
Helper and Inspiration

LIFE'S ABIDING RESOURCES

By

WILLIAM BARNES MATHEWS

Author of THE QUEST FOR LIFE

THE CHRISTOPHER PUBLISHING HOUSE
NORTH QUINCY, MASSACHUSETTS

PRINTED IN

THE UNITED STATES OF AMERICA

FOREWORD

In a peculiar sense this is your book of devotions. Differing from other such books, it seeks to bring to you a challenge. Thus, because of its various themes, it could also be a book for discussions. While it is made up of short "chapters" on many different themes, it has one underlying theme; namely, *religion is life*.

The book is the outgrowth of several years of writing; first, as an editor of a monthly Church magazine, and later, more particularly, as the writer of a regular newspaper column under the by-line of "A Minister Writes."

It has not been the purpose of the book to develop one particular subject. There are many different themes presented. For convenience and ready reference the short "chapters" have been grouped together under various headings; such as, Attitudes, Aging, Christianity, Eternal life, God, Humor, Jesus, Love, and many others.

Although the book is a collection, the underlying theme —*religion is life*—the way one lives, seeks to emphasize "Life's Abiding Resources." Beliefs, theology and philosophy are important helps to religion; but, in the final analysis, religion is the way one lives. This is especially true of the Christian religion. While there have been several great authors and teachers of religion, Jesus stands out apart from all the others in that he *was* what he taught.

Jesus did not develop a system of theology. He formulated no dogmas or doctrines. He did teach his followers about their relationship to God and their fellows. But most important, he lived a life. It is to Jesus that we must look for guidance if we are to live life at its best. In his teaching, his way, his spirit are "Life's Abiding Values."

Whatever merit these devotional themes may have, it is not drawn from the adherence to any creed or dogma or doctrine. Rather it is drawn from the life and teaching of Jesus. It is in the teachings, the life and the spirit of Jesus that we must find an authoritative guide and inspiration for living. Whether any subject in this collection deals with personal, social, moral or spiritual issue, if it has any value, any merit, any ring of authority, it is because I have continually asked myself whether it is in harmony with the teachings, the life, and the spirit of Jesus. I have not hesitated to present these themes sincerely, because in them I have found a way of life.

Readers doubtless may find some repetition. This is due to an effort to present each short "chapter" complete in itself.

The book is one person's effort to contribute clarity to the confusion in our dynamic and changing times.

William Barnes Mathews

Maitland, Florida
June, 1978

CONTENTS

Foreword 5
I. ATTITUDES — ATTAINMENT
1. Life's Abiding Resources 13
2. Life's Attitudes Are Important 16
3. When Life Tumbles In 18
4. Singing Through to Life 19
5. Overcoming Loneliness 21
6. Helping Hands 24
7. Beautiful Hands 26
8. The Great Hunger 27
9. Overcoming Life's Frustrations 29
10. Folly Is Deceitful 31
11. A Profile in Courage 33
II. AGING
1. "Senior Cits" and "Golden Agers" 39
2. You Too Can Grow Old 41
3. Growing Old Gracefully 43
4. With God You Are Never Alone 45
III. CHRISTIANITY
1. Wanted, A Truly Fundamental Christianity 51
2. The Manifesto of an Abiding Civilization 54
IV. THE CHURCH
1. The Rock of Ages 59
2. A Relevant Church in a Jet Age 61

V. CHRISTMAS

1. The Star of Bethlehem 71
2. One All Consuming Thought 73
3. Christmas, a Mystery....................... 75
4. The Challenge of Christmas 78

VI. COURAGE

1. Take Courage 83
2. Conquering Worry 85
3. Mastering Fear 88
4. Enduring Pain 89
5. Overcoming Evil 91

VII. EASTER AND THE ETERNAL LIFE

1. Passing the Torch 95
2. The Terrible Meek 96
3. Life Is Eternal (I) 98
4. Life Is Eternal (II) 101
5. The Open Door 103
6. The Conspiracy of Silence 105

VIII. FAITH

1. An Enduring Faith 111
2. An Unconquerable Faith 113
3. Faith Sets the Course of History 116
4. Something Magnificent 118
5. The Trend of the Universe 120
6. Holding to Our Integrity 122

IX. GOD

1. God in the Universe 127
2. The Will of God 129
3. Getting Through to God 131
4. How God Speaks to Us 133
5. God or Government 135
6. God's Dreams 137
7. Can Man by Searching Find God? 139

X. HUMOR

1. The Therapy of Humor 145

2. The Humor of Jesus 147

XI. JESUS
1. Jesus, a Fact in History 151
2. Jesus, the Son of God 153
3. Jesus, the Son of Man 155
4. Jesus Made Religion Relevant 157
5. Jesus' Supreme Contribution to Life 159

XII. LIFE
1. Life Is Exhilarating 163
2. Life's Fundamental Purpose 165
3. Don't Sell Yourself Short 167
4. Slow Me Down, Lord 169
5. When the Going Gets Rough 172
6. Restructuring Our Lifestyle 173

XIII. LOVE
1. The Power of Love 179
2. Love, the Conquering Power 180
3. Can Love Be Treason? 181
4. Love Is Stronger Than Death 183
5. That Without Which 184

XIV. MANKIND
1. The Measure of a Man 189
2. The Materialist 191
3. The Idealist 194
4. The Spiritual Man 196
5. The Christian 198
6. The Survival of Man 201

XV. THE NEW YEAR
1. Forward With Faith 209
2. The Perilous Power of Choice 211

XVI. PRAYER
1. Prayer Is Power 215
2. The Voice Within the Silence 217
3. Teach Us to Pray 220

XVII. RELIGION

1. What Is Religion 227
2. Religion Is Life 228
3. Man's Need for Religion 230
4. Religion and Solitude 233

XVIII. THE SPIRITUAL

1. The Quest for Spiritual Power 237
2. The Primacy of the Spiritual 239
3. Adventuring into Outer and Inner Space 241
4. Man's Inner Resources of Power 243
5. How the Spiritual Enhances Life 245

XIX. SUFFERING

1. The Fellowship of Suffering 249
2. When Sorrow Comes 252
3. Why Suffering? 256
4. What to Do About Suffering 258
5. When Suffering Persists 260

XX. TRIUMPHANT LIVING

1. The Eternal Choice 265
2. The Measure of Greatness 267
3. Turning Life's Defeats into Victory 270
4. Good Men Who Have Failed 273
5. Where There Is No Defeat 275

XXI. THE UNIVERSE

1. The Environment of the Soul 281
2. Standing on the Edge of Mystery 283

XXII. WORSHIP

1. The Worship of God 289

XXIII. CONCLUSION

1. What an Age! 295
2. The Challenge of Crisis 298
3. What of the Future? 301

SECTION I

ATTITUDES — ATTAINMENT

I. ATTITUDES — ATTAINMENT

1. Life's Abiding Resources
2. Life's Attitudes Are Important
3. When Life Tumbles In
4. Singing Through to Life
5. Overcoming Loneliness
6. Helping Hands
7. Beautiful Hands
8. The Great Hunger
9. Overcoming Life's Frustrations
10. Folly Is Deceitful
11. A Profile in Courage

1. LIFE'S ABIDING RESOURCES

Jesus is recorded to have said to his disciples, "You shall receive power when the Holy Spirit has come upon you."

In this dynamic age in which we live we have power! What are we doing with that power?

In this power-conscious age, we in America take pride in the feeling that we are the most powerful nation in the world. Are we deluding ourselves with false pride? We need to re-think this attitude. We could be carelessly neglecting our greatest source of power.

We have power. We have military power; we have the greatest military potential the world has ever seen. We have economic power; our Gross National Product grows steadily into the billions. We have scientific power; our scientists, through long and arduous research, have been developing and releasing physical power. We have technological power; our automation, computers and cybernetics lead the world. We have atomic power; we have the nuclear capacity to destroy the planet.

We have power! Or have we?

Our vast military power was unable to bring to defeat a little, poverty-stricken, oriental nation of 17 million people. Our affluent economic power seems, yet, unable to check ever-increasing pockets of poverty at home and the poverty of over-populated, frustrated "have not" nations around the world. Our scientific and technological power as yet fails great masses of people still tilling their soil in primitive fashion and eking out a wretched existence. Our abundant material resources are unable to check the decline of our inner cities and festering slums which breed disease of body and soul.

Yes, we have power! But of what use is it if it is forever to set nation against nation, if it is to be consumed in the conflict of nations and in wars of destruction, if poverty is to continue in our cities, and they continue to disintegrate, if atomic power continues as a threat of human annihilation? What will it profit us if we gain the whole world and lose life?

There is still a greater power in this universe in which we live only awaiting release to surge humanity on and up. Our vast resources of material wealth and power are of little real worth and abiding value unless under-girded and motivated by moral, ethical and spiritual values.

Only a bold, unselfish, adventurous use of the resources of power dedicated to the creative life of all humanity will set our nation on the way forward. We must refuse to follow the leadership of those who recklessly commit the resources, which nature has stored in our earth up across the ages, to destruction when they should be devoted to constructive life.

The great creative power back of this universe, God, through the mysteries of His creativity, has given us a world of unlimited resources of power. It is imperative that we soon acquire the integrity, the character, the sense of justice and the wisdom to follow God's way, else we could destroy ourselves and our world.

The eternal God is the power in which we "live and move and have our being." This creative power back of the whole cosmic order, and out of which all nature springs—in truth, without which there would have been universal emptiness—"gives to all men life and breath and all things," and is the source of victorious living. This power moves against evil; it knows no defeat. As primary power, it is eternal in the world; it surges deep within every man. Even though it is so deeply imbedded in the nature of man and the very essence of our common humanity, men seldom recognize this power. They often reject or ignore or rebel against God. However, some open up their life to this power, and those who do find themselves surged beyond the common ranks by a power which has here-to-fore been lying latent within them. They are motivated by a power not their own, the power of God.

We have seen such men of power and personality move through the pages of history. These men have made these pages sacred in the annals of men. One such man, especially, dwelt among us. His power-filled life was radiant with reality, "full of grace and truth." He was so much the "essence of life" of the Creator, whom he thought of as his spiritual Father, that many have acclaimed him as the Son of God. This Son of Man, as Jesus of Nazareth liked to call himself, so leagued himself with the spirit and power of God that he made God more real to people than ever before. Before him people knew so little of God. Now, in the life of this man all humanity has come closer to the heart of God. God's will, His way, His love stands revealed in Jesus. His power is available to all who will open up their life to His spirit.

Only as we align ourselves with the power in which we live and move and have our being, can we help to move all mankind up and on to worthy human destiny.

2. LIFE'S ATTITUDES ARE IMPORTANT

The important and decisive thing is not what happens to us as we go through life; it is how we react to what happens to us. How we face our failures and adjust to our successes, and what we make of our disappointments or our encouragements, our trials or our triumphs, our sorrows or our joys.

Our attitudes are highly important. They shape our life and determine our destiny. They shape our personality and create our character. In bringing up a child with character and personality, the attitude of the parents is as important as instruction. The latter will add knowledge to the child, while the attitude of the parents shape its personality and create its character. Attitudes are decisive in what we do and are.

Attitudes are not only important to us but also to others. Our attitudes can win for us friends or foes. They can determine other's attitudes and relationships to us. They can give a lift and an inspiration to our friends, or they can turn people away. They can brighten up the life of others with a ray of sunshine, or they can cast a shadow over another's day. The spirit of our life shapes our destiny.

Most people adopt one of three attitudes to life. With some it is an attitude of *rebellion*. They have a feeling that life is against them, that they are down on their luck. They rebel. They go about with a feeling of grievance, complaining that life has let them down, cheated them, disappointed their hopes, never really gave them what they want or what they feel should be due them. They are not satisfied with the reality of the present, or the prospects of the future. They want to turn back to the past, back to the old home, the old town, which is an indication that life has not been too bad after all had they enjoyed it as they passed along. Rebellion of this nature induces hostility, bitterness and antagonisms, even against friends. This attitude breeds dissatisfaction and loneliness and, as any doctor will tell you, is as liable to cause sickness as a germ.

Another attitude of people is *submission*. Sometimes the submission is fatalism. "To be or not to be, that is the question." The impression grows that whatever happens to us is ordained for us and that what we or any other person may do for us will never change things. Often you have heard, "It is the will of God, and I will accept it." Yet so much of what happens to us is not the will of God; and so much that happens in our world is not God's will. Rather we must seek to know God's will, and to resist that which is evil. Sometimes the submission is stoical. It has a negative and passive approach to life. It becomes easier to surrender than to strive against difficulties. To acquiesce thus is weakness. It requires strength and courage to face life's vicissitudes.

Better than an attitude of rebellion or of surrender is the attitude of *acceptance*. Acceptance is not acquiescence; it is, in reality, creativeness. With this attitude one looks for ways of making creative use of adversity and failure, of meeting suffering and sacrifice. Our failures, our disappointments and our sufferings can become the refining tools of character. The history and experience of humanity show that it requires the unsolved problems, the baffling difficulties, and the impossible situations to enable men and women to discover new and better ways. It is thus that incentive, fascination and the glory of progress has come not only to the individual but also to the human race. True acceptance is true harmony with the power in which we live, the way of God.

3. WHEN LIFE TUMBLES IN

When we lived in a New England seashore town, one of the most frequent family pleasures was to go down to the beach where our children, then young, never seemed to tire playing in the sand. Their favorite project was digging tunnels in the sand. Often, as they neared the completion of the tunnel, suddenly the sand would tumble in and the tunnel would be in ruin. But not discouraged nor defeated, unperturbed they would start again to tunnel through the sand.

Life, too, has a way of tumbling in. We are all like children playing in the sand on the seashore. Every human life, before it has gone very far, has its trials and discouragements, and many are confronted with major catastrophes. A man comes home after a visit to the doctor. He must tell his wife the bad news of a serious disease. As they sit together thinking of the plans they have had for the future, they say, "This cannot happen to us!" But it does happen. Life tumbles in.

Yes, to many of us life comes tumbling in. Aspirations and plans, which we have projected, tumble in. It may be because of some sickness or some blunder or a grevious sin or some evil through no remedial fault of our own. We can meet these with discouragement and defeat, or we can, unperturbed, begin with resolution and courage to set about our tasks of building anew.

At times, one thing after another may come in upon us. We feel that we cannot carry on. Life, for us, has tumbled in. The preacher comes and says, "Keep your courage up; hold to your faith; God will take care of you." But you say, "Those are easy words. What if He does not?" What if pain lingers on and we are confined to debilitating sickness? What if haunting sin holds us in its grasp? What if untimely death comes to a loved one? What then?

We must realize that there are some things that God does not do. He does not keep life from tumbling in. He does not do for man what man can do for himself. He does not change the orderliness of His universe even to make life easy for His most faithful followers. He sends the rain upon the just and the unjust alike. He does, however, give us, as von Hegel once wrote, "the strength and faith to grasp life's nettles." He does release inner resources of strength to those who follow His way, His wisdom and His Spirit.

If anyone was ever justified in questioning God, Jesus was. Yet we stand amazed before his matchless life. In the midst of what his world called defeat, he carried through to triumph. When on the cross, his enemies taunted him, God did not deliver him. Jesus gave up his spirit with a prayer of faith and confidence in God and God's way of life. "Father into thy hands I commit my spirit."

When for Jesus life came tumbling in, he found himself in the hands of God, his spiritual Father.

Before his crucifixion he told his followers, "In the world you will have trouble, but take courage, I have conquered the world." We, too, with faith and trust in God, can achieve triumphant lives.

Yes, we are like children playing in the sand. When the sands of life come tumbling in upon us, we, with confidence in God, must make them incentives to "tunnel through" to our life's goal.

4. SINGING THROUGH TO LIFE

When I was a student in High School, I attended a concert given in our school auditorium by a then very well-known quintette. All the singers were accomplished and very popular and greatly applauded; but the prima donna of the quintette was a young girl scarcely out of her teens. When she sang, the audience gave her prolonged applause, bringing her back to the stage again and again. How easily I, a high school boy, could have had a "crush" on this beautiful and talented girl. Often afterwards I thought of her, as I saw her that night: beautiful, happy and successful. She was a vision of happy, vivacious, care-free youth.

The years moved along, and I went to college. Later I was ordained in the ministry and went to a large city to take up my first pastorate. Soon I learned of a home in my congregation which needed a call from its minister because of a sad affair that had come to that home.

When I called at the home, I was met at the door by a young married woman, who introduced herself as a daughter of the family, and who lived in another part of the city. She invited me in. We talked casually for a few minutes about the Church, for it was her Church too. Then, the young woman drew up a foot-stool, and seated herself before me, her pastor, and brought the conversation to the point of my call. She told me not only about the present sad affair which had come to the family, but also of two others which had befallen it. There, at the feet of her young pastor, sat this young woman, relating a sad and regretful story of her family. As she spoke, gradually I recognized that the beautiful young woman sitting before me, with tears in her eyes and pouring out words from an aching heart, was none other than the beautiful, charming, successful young girl I had heard singing during my high school days. This vision of happiness I had not forgotten.

As I listened to her story, I realized that the first tragedy to befall the family had occurred at the time some years before, when I heard her singing, and had viewed with such great admiration the happiness and success which had been hers. In spite of the sad, unhappy episode in her family life, she sang her way to success and gave inspiration to others.

She continued to sing her way through to life that was beautiful and inspiring. She was especially generous with her great talent to her Church. In spite of the fact that life had tumbled in more than once, she continued to sing her way into fuller, more helpful and more inspiring life. One of the large recording companies recorded many of her songs. Were I to mention her name, some of you would remember it as well as her voice.

How little we know of the intimate life of people whose apparent happiness and success we may aspire to or even to envy. We think of the life of the Coolidges in the White House. But how their life must have been saddened by the untimely death of their son. Or the gay life of the Roosevelt family. Yet with all their outward happiness and success, how little we know of the tensions and the anguish and the discouragements which were theirs. How little, so often, do we understand the deep concerns even of our friends.

Let us be more thoughtful and charitable to all about us, for we may never know the sad, even the tragic burdens they may quietly bear. Although life may, at times, tumble in upon us, let us, too, continue to sing our way through, and to radiate inspiration and happiness and helpfulness.

5. OVERCOMING LONELINESS

Have you ever been lonely? Of course you have. All of us have been lonely. Yet it seems absurd to say this to a people who live in our modern cities. Surely, in our teeming world, no one is lonely. We are surrounded by thousands. We are crowded into apartments and condominiums. On streets and highways, at work or play, everywhere we go there are people.

Yet never alone—we are lonely! Perhaps the feeling of loneliness is never more overwhelming than when one stands on the street of a large city amid the jostling crowds coming and going. People, people everywhere! We are not alone, yet we are lonely!

The small child does not like to be left alone. Boys and girls growing up out of childhood into youth toward adulthood sensing mysterious experiences fraught with strange wonder and frightening power, often misunderstood by their elders, are lonely. Mature men and women, regardless of their resourcefulness, are often lonely. "The plowman homeward plods his weary way," the professor thinks thoughts which cannot be shared, the housewife's amenities, planned with care and affection, go unnoticed— these and many others, seeking to share the joys, the light and the happiness which have come to them, often find love's labors lost. All experience a loneliness of soul.

Older people, treading where the shadows lengthen in life's eventide, and where they were once surrounded by a host of friends, now find their ranks gradually thinning out. Here is loneliness, often tender and pleading for companionship and understanding. As old friends pass on, they are left alone in the city. There no one knows his neighbor, and at his "terminal illness" those who knew him are gone or are too far away to bid him fare well, and those who lower his body to its final resting place may never have seen his face.

The ultimate necessity, forced upon us by loneliness in our modern life, demands of us two things: first, those of us, as long as we are able, must seek to assuage loneliness wherever we may see it; and secondly, while the opportunity is still ours, we must seek to meet loneliness constructively and creatively.

Loneliness can be creative. It can become a means of strength. It can become beautiful and good. When we have come to recognize that, however good and desirable the fellowship of friends may be, it cannot take the place of fellowship with God. God alone meets the deep hunger of man's soul.

How well this has been illustrated for us by G. B. Shaw's impressive "Joan of Arc." When Joan was led to the stake, she was alone. Yet she exclaimed, "Yes, I am alone on earth. I have always been alone. Do you think that you can frighten me by telling me that I am alone? France is alone; and God is alone; and what is my loneliness before the loneliness of my country and my God? I see now that the loneliness of God is His strength; what would he be if he listened to your jealous little counsels? Well, my loneliness shall be my strength, too; it is better to be alone with God: His friendship will not fail me, nor counsel, nor His love. In His strength I will dare and dare and dare until I die."

Ever and always the messengers of love and the prophets of life have traveled a lonely road. Jesus, too, felt loneliness. He knew the loneliness of men. Although the crowds followed to hear his gracious teachings, yet how lonely! Lonely among the crowd, lonely in his own home with his mother and brothers and sisters, lonely among his own disciples. Alone in the Garden of Gethsemane, he asked his disciples, "Could you not watch with me one hour?" Yet on the cross, he held to his oneness with God. His spirit changed human history. His spirit can still strengthen and transform life for generations yet to come.

6. HELPING HANDS

The handshake, so familiar among Americans and Europeans, is a symbol of greeting and friendship. But the hand, especially the touch of your hand, can mean infinitely more; it can impart strength, courage, quiet, peace and love.

We all know the story of "The Praying Hands," and how the artist immortalized the hands which toiled that his might give unhampered release to the creative expression within him.

I had, for many years, taken the human hands for granted, until the power of the human hands was brought to my attention by a young friend. This young man had been sent by his parents to M.I.T. to study engineering. Although he had graduated with honors, I knew he would never become an engineer; his mind did not turn that way; his interests were elsewhere. He should have majored in philosophy or medicine or religion. Knowing his indecision about his life-work, I tried to interest him in the ministry. He went on to do more study.

Some years later, I learned that he was a doctor in his home town. Later I visited him there and found that he was an Osteopathic Doctor. I chided him in a friendly way for taking up a profession in which he used his hands instead of going into a profession into which he could give, as I thought, more expression to his brilliant mind. He was silent for a few moments. Then, holding out his hands, he said, "The human hands are among the most wonderful things in the world. There is a power in them which few people realize." He went on to say, "I have heard you in your sermons speak about Jesus' hands, and how Jesus laid his hands on the weary, the disturbed, the sick, and brought to them new strength and a restoration of the power to live. Jesus used his hands in his ministry to heal;

I am using my hands to heal, also, in my ministry to the sick."

Yes, there is a wonderful healing power in the touch of loving human hands. They can give health; they can impart friendliness, courage, strength, calm, peace and love.

Going back across the years in my thoughts I can recall how, when, as a child, I was sick, my father would rub my feverish brow with his rough, toil-worn hands until the pain passed away and there would come restful sleep. I recall, also, an occasion, when I was called to a hospital to see if I could minister to a sick woman who was bordering much of the time on hysteria. When I entered the hospital room, I found the woman in great mental distress. What could I do? I really did not know what to do. But, as I stood beside her bed in pity, I took her restless hands into both of mine and repeated slowly the 23rd Psalm. Before I had finished it the second time, the woman had dropped off into restful sleep. Again, when one whom I loved most dearly was tossing often in distress, I would gently caress her brow with my hands and gently close her eyes. Soon releasing sleep would come to ease her distress.

Loving human hands are wonderful! How well Jesus knew this. What helpfulness his hands brought to others. Recall the relief wrought by the trained hands of the osteopathic physician, or the skill in the hands of a dedicated surgeon. Think how a handclasp can over-power enmity, and create friendliness and love. It works both ways. In a recent letter from the wife of a physician friend who had passed away, I read these words, "I found keeping my hands busy helping others as I did in the hospital, was my salvation."

God gave you and me hands not merely to feed ourselves, but also to help others.

7. BEAUTIFUL HANDS

Hands can not only be a most useful part of one's body, they can also be a most beautiful part. Listening to soap commercials on TV one could easily conclude that to use a particular liquid soap one can be assured beautiful hands. This may not always be true. Really, much more is required to make hands truly beautiful.

Here is the secret for beautiful hands. This secret I learned from a very kind and lovely woman. She was the Principal of a New England Elementary school for many years until the day before her retirement, when she was found dead at her school desk. She was also, for many years, the Superintendent of the Junior Department, in the Church which I served.

One Sunday morning I paused for a few minutes in the Junior Department, as I often liked to do, to hear the Superintendent's worship story. On this particular morning, she told about an incident which had occurred during that week in her public school.

One of her teachers had in her room a boy—I shall call him Johnny—who always came to school with dirty hands. After repeated scoldings, this teacher finally decided to take Johnny to the Principal's office to see what could be done about the dirty hands. So, when she took the boy into the office, she said, "Miss Bliss, just look how dirty Johnny's hands are. I think they are the ugliest hands I have ever seen."

Miss Bliss looked at the hands which were stretched out before her. Then, after looking into the face of the hapless, trembling boy before her, she turned to the teacher and spoke with deep feeling.

"I do not think that these are ugly hands. Truly, I feel that they are among the most beautiful hands I have ever seen. I know why Johnny's hands look dirty. Every morning before he comes to school, he takes a sack and goes down along the railroad tracks to gather lumps of coal which have fallen from the freight cars. This coal is the only fuel that his widowed mother has to cook food for herself and her three children, and also to provide heat for their little cottage. Yes, I think Johnny's are beautiful hands."

With this story, Miss Bliss concluded her worship by repeating this Scripture text: "Man looks on the outward appearance, but the Lord looks on the heart." (I Samuel 16:7) Hands are beautiful not just by the way they appear, but by what they do. Helping hands are always beautiful hands.

You and I have felt the touch of beautiful hands. I shall—and I am sure you will also—hold in ceaseless memory beautiful hands whose touch we have felt. In countless, never to be forgotten ways their help, their sacrifice, their labor of love have blessed our life.

The labor of another's hands, as seen through love, gives these hands a beauty which can never be surpassed nor forgotten. You, too, may have beautiful hands if you remember the secret: hands are beautiful not merely by the way they look, but especially by what they do.

8. THE GREAT HUNGER

The life of mankind is filled with desires, many worthy, many unworthy. These desires are the natural expression of man's needs. They have urged man on to the fuller achievement of life. There is the hunger for food, for companionship, for sex, for love. Jesus commended people for worthy desires: "Blessed are they who do hunger and thirst after righteousness."

Desire is the great common denominator of life. We all desire something—many things. We want a better job, finer clothes, more leisure, more fun, the latest model car. If we are a worker, we want another job where the pay is more; if we are a salaried worker, we want a position where the prestige is greater and the salary higher; if a teacher, we want a school where parents and pupils appreciate us; if we are a preacher—well, the distant fields always look greener. We, all of us, always want something better. We want pumpkin pie; then we want whipped cream on it.

A noted social psychologist, several years ago, classified mankind's wants into "Four Wishes": the wish for security, for recognition, for superiority, and for new experiences. In the final analysis, our wishes may be summed up in one great desire: an adequate fulfillment of life. This is the great hunger.

Unfortunately, so often this great hunger goes unsatisfied. There are many things which hinder its fulfillment. Often a desire for the adequate fulfillment of life is thwarted by unfulfilled desires. People, having been thwarted in many of their desires, often try to get away from reality. Many resort to drink, some to drugs. They may even end up in mental collapse.

Very often the hunger for life is unfulfilled because many have the feeling that there are other desires which must be satisfied immediately. We want to live life at its best, but—. We want to be honest in business, but we want our family to have the best in everything. We want to go to college, but there is some "good money" to be made at the moment. We want the way of love and peace, but we want the security of force. We want to support religion and the Church, but there are so many other things we want first. We want to be good, but not just yet.

Again, others find the great hunger for an adequate fulfillment of life unsatisfied because of conflicting desires.

Oh these conflicting desires, how they fill our life with complexes! The noble desires seem to be in constant conflict with the lesser. There is the eternal struggle between the right and the wrong, between the higher and the lower, between the spiritual and the material. Even the Apostle Paul cried out: "I do not do the good I want, but the evil I do not want is what I do." In every one there is divinity and dust.

Mankind has many desires; but, above all, he has one great hunger which must be satisfied if he is to achieve the fulfillment of life. He wants the sense of one great reality. He wants life. He wants God. The ancient Hebrew poet expressed it thus: "As the hart pants after the water brooks, so pants my soul after thee, O God. My soul thirsts for God, for the living God." Only as one satisfies this one great hunger will he be able to achieve life at its best. This must come through disciplined living, not through some miracle. One must undertake those disciplines which will develop life in proper proportions. This was Jesus' way. He so lived that he availed himself of the spiritual resources which well up in God. He taught the accessibility of these spiritual resources to all who follow his way. "Whoever drinks," he said, "of the water that I shall give him will never thirst."

9. OVERCOMING LIFE'S FRUSTRATIONS

Psychologists have told us that of all the fateful places to reach in one's life is to come to the place where he feels, "What is the use?" When one reaches this point of utter frustration, he stands on the brink of an abyss. One step further could mean the abyss and destruction.

However, one does not need to step off into the abyss. He may have five choices before him.

1. One may accept boredom. When a person feels so thwarted by the circumstances of life which seem to enmesh him, and when he approaches the place where he feels, "What's the use?" he need not in desperation step over the brink. Many people acquiesce to the conditions surrounding them and accept boredom. They may even become drudges plodding along. Our industrialized life, which demands that multitudes of workers perform humdrum, mechanical jobs day after day on assembly lines, tend to force workers to accept this kind of futile living.

2. One may rebel. There are those who refuse to acquiesce to the frustrating circumstances of life in which they find themselves. They take the way of rebellion. Youth often rebel. They grow up in a highly complex and confused world. They are unable to grapple successfully with it. Through lack of education or opportunity, they become frustrated. They refuse to acquiesce. They rebel. Often their rebellion is violent and results in further frustration. For some rebellion may lead to a way out when tempered with wisdom.

3. One may look for an escape. Those who refuse to acquiesce in boredom, and who realize that rebellion often makes life situations worse, look for a way of escape. There are high ways and low ways of escape. Unfortunately many take a low way. They resort to drink, even to drugs. But there are high ways of escape from frustration open to those who earnestly seek after them. Some may need the help of counselors or psychiatrists, and through disciplined living make successful life adjustments.

4. One may have a nervous breakdown. These people permit themselves to reach the place where they say, "What's the use?" Their feeling of frustration overwhelms them. They seem to lack the resources to meet their frustrations successfully; but unwilling to give up and go into the abyss, they struggle on until their nerves break, and they let themselves into a physical or mental breakdown. For them the way back is difficult but not impossible.

5. *The way of religion.* Unfortunately many people do not turn to religion until it is too late. They come to their church or minister as a last resort when they have reached a point where it is most difficult for their minister to help.

There are deep inner resources in religion which can bring renewed strength to those who are willing to undertake spiritual disciplines. Too many people expect their religion to redress all their distresses and failures and mistakes by some miracle. But it is not accomplished this way. They must recall that Jesus had his temptations too; he also had his struggles. But through disciplined living he leagued himself with the spiritual resources which well up in the living God. His help came through surrender to the will and way of God. During his last night he prayed in agony, "not my will but thine be done." He came out of that prayer in full surrender to God. He placed his all in the way of God.

Those who can reach this point of surrender to the will and way of God find that they can overcome their difficulties and move up to further development of character and personality. They can live life abundantly.

10. FOLLY IS DECEITFUL

One day I was walking with a friend through the Tuilleries Gardens in Paris. We were returning from the Louvre where we had been seeing some of the world's great masterpieces of art. As we were walking through the Gardens, he asked me if I had seen the statue of Folly. I had not, so he took me along one of the walks leading to it. It stands in an open space surrounded by shrubbery. As we

approached, we had a full front view of the statue. For
several moments I stood there studying the statue. Folly
was a woman. Her dress was a long flowing robe. Her left
hand was raised to a level with her forehead seemingly
shading her face. Her other hand extended as if to welcome
one. Her face wears a look of wanton pleasure with an
enticing smile as if to lure one to her.

As I stood there studying the statue, my friend had
walked around to the other side where he bade me to
come when I was ready for another point of view. As I
walked around, I saw, from this angle, that Folly had been
holding a mask before her face. Now, as I viewed her,
her mask seemed removed, her head flung back, and over
her face there was an expression of pitiable anguish, deep-
lined with remorse and regret.

How truly symbolical! If we will but take the mask off
folly, she has nothing to offer but regret and remorse. We
may feel that she has pleasures to offer, but when we get
behind her mask, we discover that these are illusory and
deceptive.

In this connection, recall the story concerning a Persian
Monk who one day visited a confectioner in his shop. The
confectioner, wishing to honor the Monk, poured some
honey into a dish and set it before him. Immediately a
swarm of flies settled on the dish, some upon the edge of
the dish, but the greater number in the middle. The confectioner drove them away. Those upon the side flew
away with ease, but the others were prevented by the
honey clinging to their wings and, thus, they were ruined.
The Monk noticed this and said to the confectioner; "That
honey dish is like the world, and the honey as the pleasures
in it. Those who enjoy them with moderation, not having
their hearts filled with the love of them, may, with ease,
escape; while those, who, like foolish flies, have given
themselves wholly to their sweetness, will perish because
of their folly."

Let us beware of the world's honey dishes. Wanton pleasures so often make themselves attractive; but, like folly, they bring only remorse, even destruction.

11. A PROFILE IN COURAGE

With courage each of us should look deeply into the meaning of life. If we have not found a meaning of life for ourselves, we must seek until we have found a meaning satisfying to our soul.

As I have looked at life, in keeping with the judgment which I have acquired and the experiences which have come to me, I have come to feel that life has deep meaning and an eternal purpose. But mine has been a privileged life. By this I mean that most of my life has been lived as a minister; and the mission of a minister is to help other people. I have realized the truth that the giver often benefits more than the receiver. True, my life has experienced, as have multitudes of others, moments of discouragement, waves of disappointment, seasons of sickness and pain, and deep sorrow; yet, on the whole I must say with deep gratitude, "life has been good to me."

Had it been otherwise, what would I be saying? What if I were lying flat on my back unable to move my limbs as my good friend, Jim, whom I visit occasionally and whose friendship I cherish. For several years now Jim has been paralyzed from his waist down. In comparison, how fortunate I am. True, I have experienced the suffering and pain of a major coronary. The weeks dragged into months with experiences of discouragement, depression and thoughts of "Why did this have to happen to me?" But I recovered. I have had twenty intervening years of excellent health. It's easy for me to say, "life has been good to me."

When I visit Jim, he greets me from his bed with a cheery, happy face and a cordial handshake. After a fine visit, ending in an exchange of our latest jokes, and a brief prayer, I leave a better man than when I had come, challenged and uplifted by the faith and the courage of my friend.

But it was Toni that I was thinking about when I first started to write. I met her only once. I came away with a tear in my eye and anguish in my heart. Yet it was a tear of joy, and an exquisite anguish which comes to one who is deeply moved and inspired by coming into the presence of a beautiful soul.

We were on a vacation trip. We stopped in my wife's home city. She wanted to see some of her friends. But first of all she wanted to see Toni. Why Toni? By a phone call we learned that we could go out to her home and see her at once.

When we arrived to see Toni, we were greeted at the door most cordially by her husband. He had retired the year before, but with his cheerful, happy face, he seemed too young to be retired. Presently he led us into Toni's room. She was lying prone in bed. With a beautiful and lovely smile, she cordially greeted my wife; and, then, me. Instinctively I reached out my hand to take Toni's, but her hand lay motionless on the bedcover.

Yes, Toni was paralyzed from her neck down. She cannot hold the book and the letters she would read. Her husband holds them for her and turns the pages. He dials the numbers for the many telephone calls she makes. He and a friend write the letters she sends out.

On this day of our visit, they were having a "tour" of Europe. Their granddaughter was traveling there. Each day, following her itinerary, they traced, on a large map on the wall opposite her bed, the places she visited, and read with interest about these places.

I shall carry with me the memory of this visit through the rest of my days. Toni and, yes, her husband are among the most remarkable people I have known. Theirs is a life of faith and courage and inspiration. One can only hope and pray that others, who find themselves in such situations, could be as inspiring and helpful.

In spite of what has been their lot, for Toni and her husband, life did not tumble in. It has been steadily helpful and inspiring to other lives. They have been the source of countless blessings to others. They have sent out countless cards and letters to the sick and shut-ins as well as to their friends. Countless telephone calls have been made to shut-ins and, also, for their church, of which they are among the most helpful members. Each month they have supplied their church paper with a column—"Among Us Folks."

Toni's husband is devoted to her. With their friends they celebrated their fiftieth wedding anniversary. Each day by working together they do so much good. They have done it quietly to be of help to others. The multiple sclerosis came upon her gradually, until, at length, it completely paralyzed her from her neck down. She had been confined to bed for the past six years. She used a special headset when she talked over the telephone. Her husband and a friend have helped her send out the hundreds of cards and letters. The year of our visit, they mailed out 1981 cards and letters. During April, 233 letters were mailed out. Her pastor says of her, "She has a contagious faith and a great will not to give up." People who go to visit her, he says, "wind up with being strengthened themselves by her ministry."

Toni and her husband have found an inner well of strength and courage and power. In God's kind mercy and gracious love, they have lived in faith, hope and love. What a full and wonderful life. Each day has been too short for them. "We put ourselves," she explained, "in the hands of God each day, and we feel that He takes care of our days for us."

SECTION II

AGING

II. AGING

1. "Senior Cits" and "Golden Agers"
2. You Too Can Grow Old
3. Growing Old Gracefully
4. With God You Are Never Alone

1. "SENIOR CITS" AND "GOLDEN AGERS"

The assumption that "growing old" is inevitable for most of us is patently valid; like death and taxes, it's one of life's certainties. But it cannot be assumed with equal confidence that the experience of aging will always exhibit graceful characteristics. Our life's journey does not often or for long lead us "beside the still waters and green pastures"; but, like the course of a mountain stream on its way to the sea, encounters sharp boulders which thrash it into foam or dash it onto rugged walls of granite which painfully restrict its flow. So much there is in our life that "turns earth's smoothness rough."

An elderly parishioner once remarked to me, "Growing old is not fun." Even to be reminded of "growing old" sometimes hurts. As Ned Huppell has put it:

> I wish folks wouldn't take my arm
> To shield my ancient bones from harm.
> I also wish that they would stop
> Addressing me as "dad" or "pop".
> All such things, alas, remind me
> Of the years I left behind me.
> "Senior Cits" and "Golden Agers"
> Are applied to us old stagers—

> Euphemisms leave me cold.
> Why not just say that we are old?*

The causes are often clearly evident: ill-health, loneliness, unhappy memories, anxieties. These are not fun. Shakespeare stated it with stark reality:

> Last scene of all,
> That ends this strange eventful history,
> Is second childishness and mere oblivion,
> Sans teeth, sans eyes, sans taste, sans everything.

True, aging has its difficulties, but it also has its rewards. More aches and pains, perhaps, but more sympathy and understanding; fewer friends, but more deeply loved; fewer pleasures, but more deeply experienced; more loneliness, but greater leisure for skills old and new; less physical fitness, but an increasing spiritual richness. Recall the words of one of our martyred Presidents, James A. Garfield, "If wrinkles must be written upon your brow, let them not be written upon your heart. The spirit should not grow old."

"The spirit gives life." Aging, far from discouraging us with prospects of being a dead-end road darkening by diminishing prospects and hopes, can challenge us with opportunities for discoveries of new interests and new adventures. Capacities and powers long latent within us are awaiting release and development, and are surely intended by the creative God, as Jesus has affirmed, that we might have life abundant and not have it thwarted or diminished by advancing years.

This was well expressed in the early beginnings of Christianity by the Apostle Paul: "Forgetting what lies behind and straining forward to what lies ahead, I press on toward the goal for the prize of the upward call of God in Christ

---

*Hiram College Broadcaster

Jesus." This adventuring, this pressing forward for that which lies ahead, rises out of the spirit. It is looking at life with hope and with the will to adventure into the yet not fully realized, the world of mind and spirit.

Much is being written today, and much is also learned about aging. A changed attitude is altering the way we are regarding older people. The stereotypes of wrinkled and sterile figures tottering toward the grave are vanishing as everywhere we are seeing "old men dreaming dreams" and the aged mounting on "wings as eagles." It cannot be otherwise as mankind increases in intelligence and in wisdom, and as we are motivated by a creative and loving God.

2. YOU TOO CAN GROW OLD

Darling, I am growing old,
Silver threads among the gold
Shine upon my brow today
Life is fleeting fast away.

So goes the sentimental song of the oldsters.

Many of you have observed how the theatrical people age twenty-five or more years during the hour or two in which they go through some play on the stage. Their tricks of make-up, manner and voice seem almost real. Actually, actors and actresses do not hold a monopoly on the secrets of growing old in a hurry.

You, too, can grow old.

All too many men and women all about us are doing so without half trying. They are actually wasting good, productive years. They are even losing their youthful appearance and spirit as if there were some reward to be gained or something to sing about.

Too many men look forward to the age of sixty-five and

women to the age of sixty-two. They have been told, "Then, you can retire." They have been told, and have repeated themselves, such aging phrases as: "Soon you will be too old for that." "You are too old for that kind of work." "Be your age." "Those kind of games are for young people." Yes, the "senior citizen" is being thoroughly conditioned to think in terms of age.

The old Bible verse, "As a man thinks in his heart, so he is," has been explained to mean many things, but one of these is the secret of aging. Think about growing old, and you will get there fast.

Across a long span of years, I have picked up several suggestions on aging. Here are a few of them.

1. Worry about the mistakes of the past. This really will age you; it will put wrinkles on your face and furrows on your brow, for this is so frustrating. Fuss and fret, run up your blood pressure, put your nerves on edge.

2. Cross bridges before you get there. Worry about things which may never happen.

3. Brood over real or imaginary slights from family or friends. This helps to exaggerate them.

4. Conclude, when you have reached a certain age, that you are too old for gardening, hiking, golfing, teaching a Church School Class, serving on a committee, in fact for anything.

5. Nurse every ache and pain. Each heart flutter may forecast a coronary, each headache a tumor, each passing pain a cancer. Don't consult your doctor; just fret and worry about the worst.

6. Drop down in an easy chair and think how "tired and weary" you are. Drop your shoulders and the corners of your mouth and grunt and groan.

7. Deal warily with everything new; new ideas, ideas and projects, and especially truth; it could make you free. Close your mind to progress.

8. Don't try the resources which lie within religion. Religion never was meant to be a last resort.

9. Get a rocking chair, and rock your life away.

> Age is a quality of mind.
> If we have left our dreams behind,
>   And hope is cold,
> If we have ceased to look ahead,
> If our ambition fires are dead,
>   Then we are old.

> But, if from life we take the best;
> And, if in life we keep the zest,
>   If love we hold
> No difference how the years go by,
> No difference how the birthdays fly
>   We are not old.

3. GROWING OLD GRACEFULLY

In ever increasing numbers today all about us are men and women who have lived lives of usefulness, but who are now retired from their trade, their business or their profession. They now have the time to do some of the things which, through a busy work-a-day world, they never had the time to do. They are busily and happily engaged in bringing to completion some unfinished work. It may be painting a picture, writing a book, building a cabinet, the collection of specimens, even the completion of an education.

There are also others who have lived active and busy lives, and who have come to retirement with no unfinished work, no unfinished portrait, no book to write, no antique to renovate, but who, nevertheless, can serve by giving themselves in bringing hope and help into the life of others. We find them serving in their churches, in schools, and in the cultural life of their community. All these find happiness in further contributions to life, contributions in which the pay is not in dollars but in the rewards of usefulness.

I know a retired school teacher who gave her years to teaching in elementary and high school. While her teaching was her major work, she led a very busy life of helpfulness to others—to younger and inexperienced teachers, to community and to family. Upon reaching retirement, when she could have rested from a very busy life, she volunteered to teach English to foreign-born adults. Thus, her years of retirement teaching were, according to her, the most rewarding years of teaching. Her pupils were most generous in their expressions of appreciation. She reaped the rewards of helpfulness.

In our community there lives a retired college president. Before he had quite reached the age of retirement, he had to retire because of a serious sickness. Today, although living with heavy physical handicap, he is an outstanding leader in our community. He helps in every worthy community enterprise. Often he is the inspirer and the leader in these worthy projects. His only reward is usefulness.

There is a little lady who has celebrated seventy-six birthdays and who spends her days making little girl's dresses out of second-hand material for which others have no use. Already, through the United Church Women, she has given to needy children 176 dresses. It gives her something to do with her abundance of "spare time."

There are these and others—their number is legion. Most of these active and often weary retirees receive no pay for their contribution to our culture; but, at the end of a day, they seek rest knowing that they have helped. They are happy, they have their reward.

All too often we have thought of middle years and old

age as the time of waning powers and fading charm. Sometimes they are; yet in every community, we find men and women who are much more delightful companions in their later years than they were in their youth, and who are much more gracious and understanding at sixty-five than they were at thirty-five. They may lack some of the physical vigor which they had in youth, but they reveal a new ability to understand people and situations. They have, through experience, found the way to "heal the wounds of time with loveliness." They have found the magic of keeping on growing through life to the end of the journey. Down deep in their hearts they can say,

> Let me grow lovely growing old,
>   So many things do—
> Lace and ivory and gold,
>   And silks need not be new.
> There is a healing in old trees
>   Old streets a glamor hold.
> Why not I as well as these,
>   Grow lovely, growing old?"
>   *K. W. Baker*

4. WITH GOD YOU ARE NEVER ALONE

A large billboard on a U. S. Highway in our town commanded our attention and contemplation. "With God you are never alone." This reminds us of the words of Francis Havergal, the hymn writer: "Seldom can a heart be lonely if it seeks a lonelier still." In an age so confused and perplexed as ours, men and women need a sustaining spirit.

On a cold and rainy day a few years ago I was called

upon to conduct a funeral. The person whose funeral I was conducting was entirely unknown to me. All that I knew was that she had been living alone for several years in a nursing home, that she was very old and had outlived her contemporaries. At the brief memorial service, only five of us were present to bid a last farewell; her lawyer, two elderly friends, the undertaker and myself. On this dreary, dismal day, we were all moved deeply by the loneliness that in a city like Orlando, with its thousands of people, only five were found to show this act of kindness to any human being. Yet, I recall the remark of one of the elderly friends: "She may have been alone through her last years, but she was never lonely."

How true, "With God you are never alone." 'Thou hast made us for Thyself," and we are Thine. Thou art always with us. We recognize that, in the swiftly changing life of today, one of the greatest fears, especially of elderly people, is loneliness. Man was not meant by his Creator to live alone but to be a part of an ongoing fellowship. To really live is to be a part of human society. To be separated from it is unbearable.

Life has become fractured for multitudes in this mobile age; people become separated from loved ones and friends. Although they are a part of the community and the social order, the nameless crowds pass them by swiftly and indifferently. They are,

"Swift with confused alarms of struggle and flight,
    Where ignorant armies clash day and night."

In this world where so often powerful armies of nations clash, one person "alone" is overwhelmed. Even masses of nameless, friendless people only deepen the loneliness of an individual. There is no greater loneliness than being alone in a crowd.

Yet "With God you are never alone." For the person who finds and loves God, there is no real lasting loneliness. You may be alone in this world, but you are never lonely for your Father is ever present with you. God created you, God keeps you, God loves you, God is with you forever—this is our Christian faith. There is so much in this world, the home of our soul, to remind us of the presence of God.

> "The heavens declare the majesty of God,
> The whole earth displays his handiwork."
> —*Psalm*

> "Earth's crammed with heaven
> And every common bush aflame with God."
> —*E. Browning*

If we will open up our soul to God, we shall be filled with a sense of His presence. This wonderfully beautiful earth, this mysterious universe, this creative cosmos—all are manifestations of God. "Walk with bare, hushed feet upon the ground" and hear the voice of God in the call of the lark at twilight, or in the roar of the ceaseless breakers of the ocean billows on the shore. In the sunset, in a song at twilight, in the perfume and petals of a rose as you walk in the fields at any springtime, drinking in so much that lies within the soul, let the beauty of God embrace you.

To keep alive this consciousness of God in our life, we should constantly cultivate the spirit of gratitude to God for all the things great and small with which He has enhanced our life. We must not think only of ourselves, but pray for others. This is to create a community of prayer which can replace the crowd in the questing soul of modern man. Prayer is the cord which binds the soul of man with the spirit of God.

"More things are wrought by prayer
Than this world dreams of. Wherefore let thy voice
Rise like a fountain for me day and night.
For what are men better than sheep and goats
That nourish a blind life within the brain,
If, knowing God, they lift not hands of prayer
For themselves and those who call them friend?
For so the whole round earth is every way
Bound by gold chains about the feet of God."

—Tennyson

SECTION III

CHRISTIANITY

III. CHRISTIANITY

1. Wanted, A Truly Fundamental Christianity
2. The Manifesto of an Abiding Civilization

1. WANTED—A TRULY FUNDAMENTAL CHRISTIANITY

The three sessions of the Vatican Council, called by the late Pope John XXIII, and later presided over by Pope Paul VI, and having as their purpose the renewal of the Roman Catholic Church, have done much to focus the attention of Catholic and Protestant alike on the need for change in our approach to organized Christianity.

For generations the Church has placed its emphasis on a religion about Jesus, with the result that within the Church, with some exceptions, the test of one's Christianity is made in terms of one's belief about Jesus, his nature and being. The intellectual attitude toward him has been considered essential to a life of faith. Secondary emphasis, intentionally or unintentionally, has been given to the practice of the religion of Jesus. Herein lies much of the irrelevancy of Christianity for the life of today.

We recognize that the great religious doctrines are the expression of men's attempt to understand Jesus and to find his meaning for the life of their day; they express the longings of men of the past in their efforts to understand spiritual realities. Now, our concern must be to seek for the great fundamental truths which underlie the theological statements in creeds and doctrines. Our effort today must be to go beyond the interpretation of any one age or, for that matter, any church, to the fundamental truths, and to re-state these in the light of the best thinking of the day in which we live. With an ever-increasing and enlarging knowledge of life, the views of religion must grow and enlarge and expand in harmony with this knowledge of our changing and enlarging life. Creeds and dogmas of former days embodying limited conceptions are no longer adequate to the demands of an age of rapid change.

An illustration may help to clarify our thinking here. Some years ago I visited, on several occasions, the remains of the ruins of the Temple of Artemis, the Diana of the Ephesians, one of the seven wonders of the ancient world. The exact site of this temple was not known for many years until after the middle of the nineteenth century. As one delves back into the archeological study of the temple, he learns that the first shrine of worship dates back to the very early days when the inhabitants lived in villages. The life of these people centered about the shrine of the Mother-Goddess. In the eleventh century B.C., with the coming of the Ionian Greeks, the site of the city was changed. The temple of Diana, however, remained on the ancient site within a sacred precinct. Even though through the succeeding centuries, the site of the City of Ephesus changed, the temple worship remained where it had always been within the sacred precinct.

Today, as one visits the ruins of the ancient city of Ephesus, one finds these ruins over two miles further out toward the receding coastline of the Aegean Sea rather than near the site of the ruins of the temple. This is the reason why the ruins of the temple were not discovered until Mr. Wood, an English archaelogist, after long search, found them in 1867. Men had been looking for the temple within the ruins of the city, whereas it had remained in the

ancient and sacred precinct. Moreover, many temples had
been built upon this ancient and sacred foundation. As
age after age had found the temple of an earlier day inadequate to the needs of their day, they replaced the old
temple with a new temple better fitted to meet the needs
of their day. While the temple structure changed to meet
the new and expanding needs of each succeeding generation, the old foundation remained always in the sacred
precinct. Each generation erected its own temple upon the
old foundation.

So the religion about Jesus, if it is to function satis-
factory to the spiritual life of men, must be built anew on
the old foundation, to meet the needs of each new age.
As each generation finds its religion *about* Jesus no longer
adequate to meet the intellectual needs of its day, it must
replace it with another, built upon the religion *of* Jesus.
The old, the outgrown, the no longer adequate must be
replaced by the new to meet the expanding needs. The
foundation still stands, and age after age will build upon
the religion of Jesus.

Men have, too often, struggled to keep intact the old
building no longer adequate, while they have ignored the
foundation underneath. Many have failed to see that which
made Christianity vital in the beginning, that which has
weathered every storm. All too often the great concern
has been theories about Christ, while his spirit of life has
been neglected, and in the heat of controversy, ignored
and forgotten. Not theories about Jesus, but only a
Christianity like Jesus' own religion can meet the rigorous
demands of our evolving world.

The religion of Jesus is fundamental. To substitute a
religion about Jesus for the religion of Jesus is to rob
Christianity of its creative power. The history of the
Church has been very largely a history of adherence to
certain doctrines and creeds about the nature and work

of Jesus. The trend of worship has been a recitation of these creeds and an expression of loyalty to them. However, beneath all this has flowed the spirit of Jesus' religion. It has been this which has kept vital the great onward movement of Christianity.

2. THE MANIFESTO OF AN ABIDING CIVILIZATION

The ancients looked forward to a "Golden Age." Modern Americans hold before themselves the "patriot's dream" that "sees beyond the years." It is the nature of mankind to press on for the achievement of an ever new and better life.

The question arises, What are the basic principles which must undergird the building of an ever better life for mankind—an abiding civilization? If we will look carefully into the teachings of Jesus of Nazareth, we can find the manifesto for an abiding civilization. In a few pages from one of Jesus' biographers, Matthew, we find the foundation upon which an abiding order can be built.

This gospel writer, aware of the informal method of Jesus' teaching his followers, has gathered together the utterances of Jesus from various discourses and has compiled them into concise form in what has become known as "The Sermon on the Mount." Here we have a resume of Jesus' basic teachings.

The sermon on the Mount is in itself a masterpiece of expression and thought. Here in this collection of the teachings of Jesus is the very essence of Jesus' gospel, here is Jesus' Manifesto of the Kingdom of God, here in concise form is the fundamental document of Christianity, here in Jesus' teachings are the requirements placed upon all who would follow him in his quest for the way of God. It is not mere piety which impels not only the Christian but also many others who have read or heard the Sermon on the Mount to declare it the most significant of all literature in the records of mankind.

This manifesto states clearly the principles upon which human life can be fully realized. The way of life, according to Jesus, depends upon the inner spiritual resources of life. The real quest of man's life must be for the spiritual re- sources of life. The real quest of man's life must be for the spiritual, the abiding values. Man must make the way, the spirit and the life of God and His uprightness his su- preme concern, and all else will come as a natural result. Jesus' life was a full expression and a complete verification of this way. One of the distinguishing characteristics of the genius of Jesus as a teacher lies in the fact that he saw clearly—more clearly than any other great teacher—the way in which mankind can live the creative, the abundant, the eternal life. Jesus was distinguished from all other great teachers in that he lived what he taught. In his time, it was said of him; "Never spake man like this man." It can equally be said; Never man lived as this man. "In him was life, and the life was the light of men."

If mankind truly desires to build an abiding civilization, here is its manifesto. Have you ever read it carefully? You can read it through in less than half an hour.

Take half an hour out of a busy or out of a dull life, as the case may be with you, sit down with one of the newer translations of the New Testament; (the Revised Standard Version, The New English Bible, or "Good News For Modern Men") and read chapters five, six and seven of the Gospel according to St. Matthew.

If we can get the wisdom to build our common life on

this Manifesto of the Kingdom of God, we can become the creators of a great society, of an abiding civilization which can withstand the furious billows of rage and the hostilities of the ages. The forces of evil could never prevail against it, for God, our Creator, is from everlasting to everlasting.

SECTION IV

THE CHURCH

IV. THE CHURCH

1. The Rock of Ages
2. A Relevant Church in a Jet Age

1. THE ROCK OF AGES

"On this rock I will build my church and the powers of death shall not prevail against it." (Matthew 16:18) This is one of the two recorded references of Jesus to the Church.

On what rock? What is the foundation on which the Church will stand? What foundation cannot be shaken in an age of change? What will withstand the blunders and blindness, the frailties and failures of the people who make up the Church? What is the rock which can endure in this atomic age, against which not even the powers of death shall prevail?

This statement, quoted above, was made by Jesus at the close of a period when he had gone away with his disciples to a quiet place where he could concentrate on his teachings. He had been discussing with them what people thought about him. And they told him, "John the Baptist." And others said, "Elijah"; and still others, "One of the prophets."

Suddenly and abruptly Jesus turned to Peter and thrust at him the question: "But who do you say that I am?"

Simon Peter answered, "You are the Christ, the son of the living God."

Jesus answered him, "Blessed are you Simon Bar-Jona!

for flesh and blood has not revealed this to you, but my Father who is in heaven. And I will tell you, you are Peter, and on this rock I will build my church, and the powers of death will not prevail against it. I will give you the keys of the kingdom of heaven, and whatever you bind on earth shall be bound in heaven, and whatever you loose on earth will be loosed in heaven." (16:17-19)

Jesus' words here are very important. Jesus said: "You are *Petros*, and on this *petra* I will build my church." On what rock? What is the rock foundation on which the Church is to be built? Three interpretations of this statement of Jesus have given rise to three differing types of Churches.

One great branch of the Church has maintained that Peter is the rock foundation of the Church. Upon this belief a strong and powerful ecclesiastical system has been built up by the Roman Catholic Church.

Another great branch of the Church, the Protestant, maintains that the foundation rock is not Peter nor his successors, but Peter's confession: "Thou art the Christ, the son of the living God." The divinity of Jesus, so Protestantism has maintained, is the foundation rock, and upon this interpretation has built up its doctrines and ecclesiastical life.

The questing soul probes deeper to find the foundation rock upon which the Church must be built if it is to endure against all the evil forces. What was the light which Jesus saw bursting in upon Peter, and which he felt could never be dimmed, but rather continue to spread until it had also illuminated the mind and soul of men and women everywhere? To answer this question and find the truth we must go back to the simplicity and reality of the experience of Jesus and Peter, for deep beneath the doctrinal discussions about the "rock" upon which the Church is built, there lies one of the fundamental truths of Christianity; namely, in the words of Jesus, "I am in the Father, and the Father in me."

Jesus' approval of Peter was not an approval of the man nor his declaration, but of the spiritual experience of discipleship through which Peter had discovered God in Jesus. This is the rock on which the Church is to be built.

The fundamental to Jesus, that which can withstand the forces of evil and death, is a consciousness of God in life gained through the kind of life which he lived, a life consecrated to God and his fellows. Through fellowship with Jesus, through following his way, through living in his spirit, we realize God's kingdom and His way. Even as Peter discovered for himself the spirit of the living God in the life of Jesus, so must we, through discipleship with Jesus, find God.

If we can have a Church made up of men and women and youth who have undertaken this discipleship with Jesus, who have experience akin to Peter's of God-consciousness, through fellowship with Jesus and living his way and in his spirit, we shall have a Church which can meet the challenge of this atomic and space age. Even all the atomic power shall not prevail against it.

2. A RELEVANT CHURCH IN A JET AGE

I

Jesus said: "Unless your righteousness exceeds that of the scribes and Pharisees, you will never enter into the kingdom." Let us as Christians, today, ask ourselves whether the righteousness of our Churches is relevant to the dynamic age in which we live.

We are in the midst of a rapidly changing period in the

history of mankind. In the last decade alone, the scientists tell us, we have discovered more and progressed faster than in the preceding 19th century.

The jet-like pace of scientific knowledge and technology is speeding mankind on to the threshold of a future which is beyond the dream of the ages. Through marvelous advances in medical science, once dreaded diseases can be cured, pain alleviated, greater physical well-being achieved, and even the long-secret key to the origin of life is all but in the grasp of man. Through man's scientific genius, distances have been dwarfed, time modified, and the exploration of space well under way. Through man's knowledge and use of radar, transistors, computers and other intricate instruments, the knowledge of the expanding galaxies come ever nearer. Dreams and fantasies in the minds of men yesterday become the realities of today. Awesome as all this may seem, it is matched by man's infinitely ranging mind. Thus man has come up and on a long way through the unnumbered generations from the dim, distant nights, when, huddled around some fire in a cave, impulses and longings began to stir within him, to our generation which stands in the dawn of a new and greater epoch in the life of man.

In just a few years we have been thrust forward from one age into another. We have moved from the age of the cannon to that of the atomic bomb and nuclear power, from the age of the piston motor to that of jet propulsion, from the age of the airplane to that of the space satelite, from the age of the adding calculator to that of the electronic computer, automation and cybernetics. We cannot expect anything else than that, with such a rapid leap forward from one age into another, there will be massive social, political—even moral change.

Amid this rapid, changing, revolutionary world there is

a disturbing restlessness.   It creates confusion and dis-
sension.   It is not merely the problems arising out of the
East-West conflict, however real and critical these are; it
goes deeper.   Basically, it arises out of the ever accelerating
advance of secularism; for secularism, although very
attractive, is, today, in a very subtle way, a serious threat
to the advance of our social order.

II

Secularism is a way of life in which there is no need for
what men, through the ages, have thought of as religion.
Its advance proceeds deliberately without concern for
religion.   It not only feels no concern for a concept of God
but often is hostile to this concept.   Its total reliance is
upon the objective world; it has no need for the unseen.
Its temples are laboratories and factories.   It makes the
familiar and traditional forms of worship difficult, because
it eliminates the traditional object of worship, God.   The
present advance of secularism is a powerful force in the
world in the West and in the East alike.

This increasing advance of secularism is understandable;
in it there is much good.   It has much—not all—to do
with the building of the world as we know it.   It has made
living more attractive and less burdensome.   It has challenged the inventive genius of men.   But its successes have
so challenged the minds of men and so equipped his hands
as to make him feel that he—without God—can bring in
the abundant life on earth.   But scientific and technological man, in his enthusiasm for all this progress, has
forgotten the fact that man's relationship to the objective
world is not the whole of life.   Secularism errs when it
proceeds on the assumption that it is.   And in this error it
will fail to move mankind on to worthy destiny.

III

There is much more than just this objective world. Beyond this material universe is the great mystery of time and eternity. But deeper still, beyond unfathomable time and eternity, is life, and especially human life and spirit. What is life; what is the meaning of it all; what is its purpose; what is its destiny? These are the questions which only that which we think of as spiritual can answer. The notion that God is not a factor in the objective world and in the inner life of values rules out the quest for life's deepest meaning and purpose. There is at the heart of things a creative power—call it by whatever name you choose—men through the long centuries have called it God.

Today's unprecedented material advance and the resulting secularism presents the Church with an almost overwhelming challenge. When it is recalled that many of our religious beliefs were formulated before the far-reaching knowledge of the expanding universe became available not only to the man in the street but also to the scholar, we are moved to ponder the words of J. B. Phillip's book title, "Is Your God Too Small?" God is to be thought of no longer as the God of a "chosen people" nor as a one-planet deity. He is the God of the universe which is said to be infinite, without beginning, without end!

IV

Many Church leaders are questioning whether religion and the approach which it makes is adequate to the needs presented by the perplexing problems arising out of the revolutionary changes taking place. Let us recall some of these changes. The mere mention of them reminds us of the problems they present: the marvelous scientific and technological advances, the reevaluation to which moral standards are subjected, the prevalence of poverty and the inadequacy of education, the terrifying increase in lawlessness, crime and violence, the ever accelerating growth of cities, the threatening collapse of community life and disintegrating ghettos, the premature birth of nations, the tragic and irrational conflict between nations, and the ever-impending threat of nuclear annihilation. These challenge the minds of men for solutions which cannot long be delayed.

V

The question of the relevancy of religion is far from academic: Is the Church and the kind of religion it gives adequate to the problems of redemption in its tragic and gigantic setting in modern life?

As I see it, in order for Christianity to become more relevant, the Church must, among others, do two major things: (1) It must join man's search for truth and knowledge; (2) It must become more deeply, more passionately involved in life.

(1) So much of our religious thought and practice is so removed from reality that modern man is often alienated from the Church. The Church must never stand in the way of worthy progress. It must rejoice in every advance of knowledge and in every worthy achievement in science. Jesus said, "You will know the truth, and the truth will make you free." Many of the creeds, dogmas and theology, which once served the intellectual needs of men, are no longer meaningful to the outer and the inner needs of men's life today. There must be an unceasing search for the truth in all areas of life. The major emphasis of today's search has been confined to our objective world. Commendable as are the researches in the physical forces and

the material realms of life, they must not be given precedence over the fundamental moral and spiritual areas of life. The Church must set up its laboratories and research centers. It was the great electrical wizard, the late Charles Steinmetz, who said: "When men understand the spiritual power that is in the universe and gear to it, life will change for the better and move forward at a prodigious rate."

How little we know about the spiritual! There is so little known of the inner life of man. It is here that the Church must lead in research; research in mental illness which distorts sex, causes delinquency and crime; research in nervous tensions and diseases of the mind which cause greed, hatred, lust for power, war and violence; research in the causes of racial prejudice and man's inhumanity to man. These are deep Christian concerns. In an age of confusion and anxiety, the Church must minister more adequately to the mind and soul of people. It will be wise to take seriously the words of Jesus, "I am the way, the truth and the life."

(2) If the Church is to become more relevant, it must become more deeply, more passionately involved in life— in all the affairs of the life of people. Jesus said, "Not everyone who says 'Lord, Lord' will enter into the kingdom, but he who does the will of my Father." Again, he portrayed God as saying: "As you did it unto one of the least of these my brethren, you did it to me."

The mission of the Church, like the all-consuming passion of its Author, must always be "that men may have life and have it abundantly." Wherever life is thwarted, wherever there is inequity, injustice and disregard for human rights, wherever fanatical men usurp the rights of others, wherever God is forgotten or ignored—here is the business of the Church. Churches must not acquiesce nor retreat when men, motivated by a lust for power, materialism or greed, cry at them to "mind their own business." If the Church remains silent when great wrongs go unrighted, it ceases to be the Church of Christ.

It is not enough just to keep beautiful churches open for worship. Although it must be said emphatically that the worship of God in Church on Sunday is the most important thing in the life of a nation. Yet, it is idle to recite proper creeds, pray proper prayers, sing soothing songs if we are to remain apathetic to the pulsating life of our world.

Above all, if our Christianity is to meet the exacting demands of this dynamic age, it must embody the spirit of its Author. He lived God's spirit in human life. He involved himself in the affairs of men. He took compassion upon the multitudes. His all consuming purpose was that men "may have life and have it abundantly."

> "He dreamed that every soul on earth
> Should worship God . . . .
> He dreamed that every earth-born child
> Should have its rights: a happy birth,
> Love's guiding care through youth's hard years
> To manhood's dawn. He dreamed that fear
> Should have no part in human fate,
> That love should cleanse all hearts from greed and hate
>
> He dreamed his dreams, and wrought as best he knew;
> He dreamed, and God will make his dreams come true."
> —*Thomas Curtis Clark*

It was not easy. It is not easy. Men of greed and power nailed Jesus to a cross. But his life marked the turning point in the history of mankind. His spirit still points the way to the fulfillment of worthy human destiny.

SECTION V

CHRISTMAS

V. CHRISTMAS

1. The Star of Bethlehem Is Still Shining
2. One All Consuming Thought
3. Christmas, a Mystery
4. The Challenge of Christmas

1. THE STAR OF BETHLEHEM IS STILL SHINING

In this space-conscious age the Star of Bethlehem has taken on added luster. What was this star which guided the Wise Men to Bethlehem? Probably the most accepted explanation in our space-thinking day is that it was a super-nova, a new star which flared up in a celestial explosion.

Once or twice about every thousand years such celestial phenomena have occurred. When a star becomes a super-nova, its brilliancy may increase a thousand million times as, in a cataclysmic explosion, it burns itself out. The last two were in the years 1572 and in 1604.

Most astronomers now surmise that the Star of Bethlehem was a super-nova. They are now able, through celestial observation and calculation, to determine how far away a super-nova is for its brilliancy to be compared to a planet such as Venus. Astronomers have estimated that the light of the Star of Bethlehem traveled 3,000 light years (eighteen million billion miles) before it was seen on earth. With a few moments reflection we realize that was before the Pharaohs built the pyramids.

In imagination go back 3,000 light years. This star, scarcely visible, without warning, within minutes, changes noticeably, and within an hour is blasting off quantities of exploding gas at a million miles an hour. Within a day it is shining with much greater brilliancy than any other sun.

Now consider this light which, moving at the speed of light—186,000 miles per second—outward into all surrounding space, in four or five years has reached the nearest star. If there were planets encircling this star, like the planets about our sun, they would be illuminated for a few days or weeks until the light had passed on beyond. Century after century it must have shown past thousands of worlds, inhabited or uninhabited, before its light reached our earth and was seen by the ancient astronomers on their way to Bethlehem.

Moreover, the Star of Bethlehem is still shining! No longer visible here on earth; but, visible to other planets in the universe, it is still flooding its light throughout infinite space. This Christmas it may still be shining in the sky of many worlds. Any watchers in these worlds will still see its appearance and be fascinated by it as were the Magi. For centuries to come the light of the Star of Bethlehem will be ebbing out into space, and its brilliancy will still have power to bring wonder to all who behold it whoever and wherever they are.

Yes, before the light of the Star of Bethlehem fades out in infinite space, we shall have shared it with perhaps millions of other worlds. To many of those who saw it before it was seen on earth, it was even more brilliant and wonderful than when seen by the Wise Men.

What did these worlds make of it? What are other worlds making of it? Will it bring to them good tidings of great joy?

Our world has seen in it the creation of a new calendar of time, the beginning of a new era in the history of humanity, the hope of all the years to come through Him who was born in Bethlehem on the night of its appearing, and who has taught that the way of life is the way of love with "peace and good will among men."

Throughout the vast infinity of time and space wherever the creativity of God is at work, may all worlds find in it tidings of great joy. May the creative God, the Power which holds the planets and stars in their course, the spiritual Father of all men, grant that it may fill all worlds with great good and joy and peace and good will. May the Star of Bethlehem ever illuminate with its glory and significance the souls of humanity everywhere.

2. ONE ALL CONSUMING THOUGHT

As Christmas season approaches each year many of us begin to think about Christmas shopping. But there is another more important, oft recurring almost universal thought: peace in our world. We all want it. We are greatly confused as to how to get it. So, in this Advent season, a worthy suggestion would seem to be that we all give more thought to peace than to shopping. If we will think hard about ways to peace, pray for it more sincerely, express it more fully, and work tirelessly, peace will more speedily be achieved. Let this thought of peace become our earnest purpose.

It seems altogether fitting that, at this season which commemorates the coming of the Prince of Peace, we should dedicate our lives to the task of bringing "peace on earth and good will among men." Only so shall we move closer to that time when our world will be spared the scourge of war with all its reeking retinue of destruction, brutality and death. Only then shall we realize the God-ward dream:

"Down the distant future,
Through long generations,
The echoing sounds grow fainter
     And then cease.

And like a bell,
With solemn, sweet vibrations
Comes the clarion call,
Peace."

Is peace always to remain a quest far into the future? Is it to remain a dream of men? The ancient Hebrew sang:

"He shall judge between many people,
   And shall decide for strong nations afar off;
And they shall beat their swords into plowshares,
   and their spears into pruning hooks;
Nation shall not lift up sword against nation,
   neither shall they learn war any more."

(*Micah 4:3*)

Before the birth of Christ, Virgil, the Roman poet, wrote a beautiful poem celebrating the birth of a child who would bring peace and abundance to the earth. His "Fourth Eclogue" is so lofty in thought and expression, so like the Bible in its promise of redemption, we do not wonder that the poet was later hailed as a Christian prophet, and his verses acclaimed as a prophesy of the birth of Christ.

"The last great age, foretold in sacred rhymes,
Renews its finished course; Saturnean themes
Roll round again; and mighty years, begun
From their first orb, in radiant circles run.
The base degen'rate iron offering ends;
A golden progeny from heaven descends."

He goes on to describe "the lovely boy with his auspicious face," and to predict that, through his wisdom and power, misery and crime shall disappear.

"The jarring nations he in peace shall bind,
And with paternal virtues rule mankind," . . . .

that peace and plenty shall everywhere prevail, and cities

shall dwell safe without walls. The poet hails this coming one as a son of the gods.

We cannot help feeling that he drew his vision from acquaintance with the inspired words of an Isaiah or a Micah, or from the same source from which the prophets drank, the spirit of the eternal God whose providence provided for mankind a Prince who can lead men to peace and good will.

3. CHRISTMAS, A MYSTERY

Christmas is a mystery. In its origin it is surrounded by stories which make an explanation difficult. But even more unexplainable is the manner in which its celebration has come up out of the past. The many and various ways in which it is observed, the modern commercialism of the day, the stereotyped celebrations are far removed from the origin and the basic meaning from which it came. Its meaning has been so blurred that Christmas has become a holiday rather than a holy day.

In order to penetrate the mystery of Christmas, and to understand its meaning, we must look carefully at the stories in our New Testament out of which our observances of Christmas came. What are the facts? What is the truth which these stories seek to express?

There are two stories, one in Matthew's gospel and the other in Luke's. One tells the story of the three Wise Men from the East who, following a star, came to Bethlehem and found the child Jesus and worshipped him as King. The other tells of the lowly shepherds who, keeping their flocks by night, hearing heavenly voices singing "Glory to God in the highest," and obeying instructions, came to Bethlehem to find the babe lying in a manger.

These exquisitely beautiful stories (they are more than

myth) were meant to explain an event and to express in a dramatic form the meaning back of the event. They are too strange to be fiction and too sublime to be history. They have been treasured as an attempt to reveal the amazing mystery of the spirit of God in human life, especially God revealed in Jesus. They seek to tell of an event in time which is so fraught with meaning that it cannot be effectively conveyed in literal terms. There are often depths of meaning which no human mind can grasp if expressed only in words. Only as there is also evoked in the soul an emotional response can it be fully grasped. Few minds can fully comprehend an intellectual exposition of the doctrine of the incarnation, but few are those whose hearts do not respond to the beautiful, moving imagery of Matthew and Luke.

It is, however, in the stately solemnity of the opening paragraph of the Gospel According to John that we gain a fuller understanding of the way the eternal spirit of God dwells in human life. Here is a glimpse into the awesome depths of God's being; here is a hint of the source and the destiny of human life; here is the opening of the mystery of the life that was and is to be.

"In the beginning was the Word (or to use the Greek word "Logos," which in the Ephesian philosophy, means the "Essence of Life," and John's gospel came out of the Ephesian circle) and the Essence of life was with God and the Essence of Life was God . . . and the Essence of Life became a human being and dwelt among us." In this way the author of the Gospel According to John, written understandably for the people of the Greco-Roman world, identifies Jesus with God, the Creator, the Essence of Life. This is the truth which the gospel writers are seeking to express; namely, in Jesus, God's spirit is revealed in all its creativity and majesty, in all its beauty, goodness and love.

The Essence of life became flesh that man may behold the glory of God, "full of grace and truth." Here is a glimpse of the Eternal, an unveiling of the way the spirit of God enters into the affairs of men: through the life of man, especially the Man. In Jesus we see God in human life. Here is a hint of spiritual personality: man yet to be. What a foretaste of human destiny.

When we unwrap all the tinsel from about the celebration of Christmas, when in our mind and heart we reject the commercialism which has enveloped the whole Christmas season, and when in the quest of our own soul we rise above the formal liturgies repeated religiously year after year in our Churches, then we shall lift Christmas up out of the mystery which surrounds it and distorts its meaning; then, and then only, will Christmas become a spiritual experience enhancing life.

To all who share this experience, it will help to keep alive the faith that God is in life and that His holy spirit dwells within the soul that freely opens up to Him. It will remind us that He is intimately concerned with His creation. It will remind us that our origin is in Him. It will renew our joy as participants in His creative purpose. It will project man on to worthy destiny.

St. Matthew, in his story of the birth of Jesus, has given us a phrase which proclaims the mission of Jesus, but it also gives to our modern world the real, the true meaning of Christmas. He writes: "And his name shall be called Emmanuel," and he adds, "which means God with us."

Thus Christmas no longer needs to be a mystery. It enhances life's meaning and purpose. It challenges us to a realization of the intimate relationship of God and Man. Jesus could say, "The Father and I are one." We, too, are God's children. His spirit dwells in us. "You are the temple of God and God's spirit dwells in you."

4. THE CHALLENGE OF CHRISTMAS

Each year we approach Christmas with its message of good will and peace, and with the hope that, in its spirit, we can face the challenge of our dynamic age with courage and faith.

"The true light was coming into the world, but the world, though it owed everything to him, did not comprehend this. He came and those rebellious against God received him not. But to those who opened up their life to his spirit, and who gave their allegiance to him, he gave the power to become the children of God.

"So, the Essence of Life became flesh and dwelt among us, a life full of radiance and truth. We beheld him; he was radiantly glorious, such gracious glory as to become the Father's beloved Son."

"From his revealing life we have all received boundless and gracious enrichment . . . . No one has ever seen God; now in the life and spirit of this Man, God's Beloved Son, who comes nearest to the heart of the Father, God is revealed." (See St. John 1:1-18)

This is the meaning and message of Christmas. What help does it offer to our confused and baffled modern world? What hope has it for the security, the peace and the good will among the nations of men which move from crisis to crisis in this dynamic jet age.

If, as the Psalmist once wrote, man is created "a little less than God," and, as Jesus taught, a being in whom the spirit of God can dwell, then our highest social aspirations and our fondest dreams of human destiny have hope of fulfillment. Then, indeed, we have the Essence of Life working creatively with us, for, while "with man it is impossible, with God all things are possible."

For the spirit of Christmas is the hope of a civilization yet to be. Like the early Christians, we must live in an atmosphere of expectancy as of something immense, something impending, of a profoundly creative change in the progress of humanity—a faith that the dream of the ages can come true.

Thoughtful and dedicated men and women in all areas of life, people of spiritual discernment everywhere feel that the time has come in the long struggle of humanity up through the ages when mankind must make a supreme effort to move up to higher and more worthy levels of being, or else sink back toward the clod, or drift into the final cataclysm.

Too long have men given way to selfishness and hatreds and enmities, to an all-prevailing passion for material existence. To the multitudes this seemed to be the easy way. It is the broad way which leads to frustration, suffering, cruelty and, in the end, to destruction. To turn humanity toward a more worthy destiny, mankind must continue to rise from the old order and, with renewed intelligence and dedication, develop the moral, ethical and spiritual qualities of life. Mankind having, in this dynamic age, risen to such commendable and magnificent heights, must not take the broad way that leads to ignoble destruction; but, with renewed effort, continue up the narrow, the hard way to worthy human destiny and life.

The God of the universe, with His beneficent, creative power, has endowed mankind with an infinite range of the human mind capable of discerning good from evil, and creating love rather than hate, and peace and good will rather than enmity. Only as man commits himself to the power in which he "lives and moves and has his being," only as he lives in harmony with the laws of the creative, the eternal God of the universe, will he enter into his rightful heritage, and his worthy destiny.

SECTION VI

COURAGE

VI. COURAGE

1. Take Courage
2. Conquering Worry
3. Mastering Fear
4. Enduring Pain
5. Overcoming Evil

1. TAKE COURAGE

"In the world you will have trouble; but take courage,
I have overcome the world."

—Jesus

Have you ever been discouraged? It is the exception to
find one who has journeyed far into life and has never
passed through the clouds of discouragement.

How well Jesus knew this. He warned his disciples to
keep their courage up.

Many have dreamed their dreams only to have them
fade away in disappointment. Some have saved for the
closing years of their life only to have their savings swept
away by some unforeseen circumstance. A couple have
worked hard and planned for happy years together, then
death comes to take one away. An affectionate love
turns cold, leaving only bitter loneliness. Yes, "castles
built in the air" tumble down often through no remedial
fault of our own.

When circumstances of life come to prevent the realization of cherished hopes and dreams, what then? Here is
where religion may help us. In the life of Jesus we have
the inspiring and challenging example of one who lived
victoriously in spite of all that came to him. He, too,
dreamed his dreams—dreams of the kingdom of God.

His dreams were thwarted. As he faced repudiation of his understanding of God and His way, rejection and impending denial and death, he moved on with courage and confidence in God. He might have been king, but he chose the way of the cross. Because of his courageous spirit that Cross has become to all ages of Christians the symbol of triumph beyond tragedy. He has become the inspiration for those who have had their hopes shattered.

A great company of men and women challenge us to rise triumphantly above disappointment and even tragedy. The Apostle Paul was one of this company. He was beaten, stoned, shipwrecked; he was so maltreated that he was often near death; he endured all manner of dangers, in toil and hardship, through many a sleepless night, in hunger and thirst, often without food, in cold and exposure; yet amid it all, he pressed on in his high calling because he had caught the spirit of Jesus. Even in prison awaiting death, he continued to send out his letters to inspire courage and faith. George Washington Carver, in spite of slavery, poverty and abuse, pressed on to become one of America's great benefactors. Madame Curie, in spite of hardship, bereavement, poverty and sorrow, completed her experiments. Dr. Trudeau, in spite of weakness and sickness, built his hospital to help others. These, in spite of the difficulties they endured, took courage and overcame.

So we in the spirit of Jesus should take courage and, with whatever we have, give to life our best. We must press on to grasp the opportunities which await us in spite of any limitations which surround us. Our world can never become so restricted that we cannot hold to our ideals and continue to dream, if we will, like Jesus, make the supreme surrender to the wisdom and will of God.

John Kendrick Bangs once wrote a poem which can portray the opportunities which await those who maintain an inner courage.

If there is no sun, I still can have the moon,
If there is no moon, the stars my needs suffice.
Or if these fail, I have my evening lamp,
Or—lampless—there's my trusty tallow dip.
And if the dip goes out, my couch remains
Where I may sleep, and dream there's light again.

2. CONQUERING WORRY

"Do not worry about tomorrow."
                                        —*Jesus*

"Don't worry" is the easiest advice one can give. It is the most often used excuse to relieve us from the problem of a friend, and the ready made answer to anyone for whose problem we have no solution to offer. We so easily dismiss another's problem, with "Don't worry." While "don't worry" is easy advice to give, it is not easy to follow. Nevertheless, this is sound advice if sincerely given.

Too many people drift into the habit of worry. It is as a farmer once said, "If it were easy being a farmer, everyone would be moving to the farm." So, if it were easy to be free from worry, no one would worry. Freedom from worry demands disciplined effort.

Insurance companies place heart failure as the number one killer, but the cause of mortality goes deeper than that. Worry is the greatest killer of all. Dr. Charles Mayo wrote, "Worry affects the circulation, the heart, the glands, the whole nervous system and profoundly affects the health. I have never known a man who died of over-work but many from over-worry."

The habit of worry exerts a devastating strain upon one's thinking and attitude. A psychologist with a sense of humor has drawn up a helpful "Worry Chart" which has helped many to tackle their worries realistically. He classifies worries as follows:

1. Worries which never happen	40%
2. Worries about decisions in the past about which we can do nothing	30%
3. Worries about possible sickness and breakdown	12%
4. Worries about children and friends	10%
5. Worries which have real foundation	8%

The obvious point of the chart is that one should confine one's self to the few worries in the fifth group. Thus, one may be free from 92% of worries, or free from worry 92% of the time. What a relief!

Of course, it is not all that easy. We must discipline ourselves intelligently to limit our worries to those which are justifiable. Toward these we must take a positive and realistic attitude. All sickness is not imaginary, and old age is inevitable; but a positive attitude toward such as these can make life more healthful and wholesome.

Samuel F. B. Morse, who was confronted with many trying difficulties in his work, had this bit of advice to give: "Knowing from long experience from whence my help came in hours of difficulties, I soon disposed of all my cares and slept as sound as a child." A wholesome inner attitude is always much more important than the outward circumstances with which we are often confronted.

John Oxenham has passed on this most helpful prayer:

> Lord, when on my bed I lie
> Sleepless, then to Thee I cry:
> Put my anxious thoughts on Thee
> And on Thy dear charity,
> Make my worried prayer—and then
> Turn myself to sleep again.

Furthermore, we must refuse to borrow trouble from the future, and we must refrain from magnifying it. We must live our best today for today. We can be helped greatly in overcoming our worries by a faith in God and seeking an understanding of how He is a vital factor in our life. Jesus, the master in living, emphasized this positive trust in the guiding providence of God. He taught the people of his day, "Do not worry about life." Yet, how well he knew human life and its heartaches and anxieties. He knew what it took to put the world to bed at night and to get it up and off to work the next morning. "So," he says, "do not worry about tomorrow, for tomorrow will have worries of its own. Let each day be content with its own ills." He enumerated many things in life about which people are anxious: what they will eat or drink or what they will wear. He reminds the people about how God cares for the birds of the air, and how beautifully he clothes the flowers of the field; and he goes on to point out that, since man is of much more value than these, God will care for man. ". . . your spiritual Father knows well what you need."

God through the unfathomable mysteries of creation has provided a universe of unlimited resources. Therefore, as we trust Him, many of our anxieties will fade away. Jesus urges that men must not let their lives be consumed by trifles. There are great concerns which will lift man up and surge him onward. "Set your mind on God's kingdom and his righteousness before all else," said Jesus, "and all else will come to you as well."

Dare to rest in God's kindly care,
Dare to look confidently into His face,
Then launch thyself into life unafraid!
Know that thou art within thy Father's house,
That thou art surrounded by His love,
Thou wilt become master of fear,
Lord of life, conqueror even of death.
—*John Hoyland*

3. MASTERING FEAR

"Perfect love casts out fear."
—*I John 4:18*

Ours is a fear-full world. Fear haunts the minds of men. Fear retards man's progress. It checks the avenues of aspiration. It keeps gnawing away at the hope of the world. Everyone, in one way or another, faces the problem of fear. Fear runs so far back in human heritage and takes such forms that few escape it.

Fear is not all bad. There is a reason, a purpose for fear in life. It can be a life preserver. The frightened deer can run more swiftly. Primitive man survived because of fear. We cannot dispense with fear in modern life. It keeps humanity alert. Fear of disease, of ignorance, and of evil has had its rewards. Wholesome fear not only guards a man from destruction, but also drives him to constructive effort. We must not fear fear; we must know our fears. "Education," says Anglo Patri, "consists in being afraid at the right time." Realistically speaking, we should seek to master our fears rather than to conquer them.

Fear must be mastered. Fear affects the very foundation of life. The basis of fear is the loss of faith in life, in God. This is the great lesson taught by one of man's most ancient stories. Adam, when he had sinned in the Garden of Eden, said to God: "I heard thy voice and was afraid." When man turns away from the ways of God, the first thing he meets is fear, fear of being found out, fear of consequences, fear of disaster. Fear drains a man of courage. On the other hand, men of faith are unafraid; they are men of courage. The Apostle Paul was a man of faith. Truly he could say, "I can do all things through Christ who strengthens me." In a deep religious faith lie the resources giving mastery over fear.

"Perfect love casts out fear." How can love cast out fear?

Our world situation can give us a vivid illustration of this truth. We distrust and fear Russia. Russia fears the United States. The United States fears China. China fears the United States. Russia and China fear each other. Even former friendly nations fear each other. Many in America are afraid to adopt a treaty to ban nuclear weapons, even to restrict them. Nations are haunted by fear. Fear of atomic bombs, fear of nuclear attack, fear of economic supremacy by others, fear of loss of prestige—these are a few of man's many fears. Fear breeds hate. What we hate we wish to destroy. So we build up armaments in all nations that we may rid ourselves of fear.

But only love can cast out fear, for love is intelligent good will. Only intelligent good will in the affairs of nations will bring security and peace to our common humanity. It is not inevitable that our age, so latent with possibilities, should be prostrated by fears of an atomic age if men will bend their minds and wills in a supreme effort to create good will. Men must be willing to spend their billions for good will as they have been willing to spend their billions for bombs.

The trend of the universe is on the side of good will; for God, "the power in which men live and move and have their being," is love, and "love never fails." Fear need not always haunt us. Hope lies eternal in the heart of man. Greater life is yet possible if men will align themselves with God, who is love, and perfect love casts out fear.

4. ENDURING PAIN

"Hope in God; for I shall yet praise him,
     my help and my God"   —*Psalm*

Why pain?

At the outset let it be clearly understood that this is only a partial, an inadequate answer to the question,

"Why pain?" There are pains which pass away, and there are pains which never pass away. These latter demand a more satisfying answer than is given here. Pains suffered from diseases for which medical science has as yet no cure demand courage and fortitude. They place a strain upon one's faith. They may even rob one of hope.

It does not help much to say that pain serves a useful purpose. Bodily pain is a warning that something is wrong. By isolating the pain, the physician is able to locate the difficulty and suggest a cure. Nor does it help to say that pain has been the basis of much progress. Life is challenged by pain. Pain, such as of hunger and of cold, prod men on to further achievement and progress.

Like many of you, dear reader, I, too, have felt excruciating pain. Together with the excellent physical help given me by medical science, I found further strength and courage to endure in a supreme surrender to the merciful, creative Power to which I owe my breath, my very life itself; in a complete commitment to the hands of a loving God.

Out of the experiences of pain and anguish and suffering, life has taught some of us most helpful and valuable lessons. Grace Noll Crowell has expressed this so beautifully in her exquisite poem, "Fellowship," which—lest you have not read it—I pass on to you.

> I think that I can truly say today
> That I am glad
> For all the sorrow I have had.
>
> I came upon one weeping by the way,
> And I had words to say
> To comfort her, because I, too, had known
> A sorrow that my heart had borne alone.
>
> I know that I am glad that pain has stayed
> A while with me,

For through it I learned sympathy
With every fellow mortal, hurt, dismayed,
Who prayed as I have prayed
For quick release, and then have turned to wait
The answer that will come, though soon or late.

Oh, it has taken longer than it should
For me to see
That grief and pain might work in me
Some ultimate reward, some lasting good,
I did not dream it could.
But now I know that only through these things
Can we reach out and touch Life's hidden springs.

Deep within the resources of religion lie the "hidden springs" of strength and courage awaiting to be tapped by all who make the supreme surrender to God.

Even in life's darkest moments we may cry:

"Why are you cast down, O my soul,
    and why are you disquieted within me?
Hope in God; for I shall yet praise him,
    my help and my God."

5. OVERCOMING EVIL

"Do not be overcome by evil, but overcome evil with good."
                                        —*Romans 12:21*

The problem of evil is one of the most difficult for Christians. While we may approach the problem with some answers, we do not have all the answers. Aside from the evils suffered by man as a result of natural disasters, most evil in life is caused by human beings.

Within the limits of his natural and social environment, man has the freedom to make his decisions and express himself. It is this power of choice which distinguishes man from other animals. Man may choose or reject morality and religion, or social and political orderliness. When his choices are against the moral, the ethical, the unselfish, there results human suffering. Thus, man's selfishness, his inhumanity and his sin are the chief cause of evil.

The Judeo-Christian ethics and religion hold that human beings are responsible for most of the damage done other humans. In one way or another, when we violate the moral and also the spiritual laws by our economic, social and political policies and practices, this disobedience, whether willful or in ignorance, results in the evil which befalls us. This is why Christianity holds that God does not send trouble, why God does not send evil, why God does not cause wars; men cause evil and wars.

The answer to the question, Why does God permit man's inhumanity, is this: given man's freedom, and given the moral order of our world, how could God do otherwise? The answer would have to be that God could prevent evil by destroying man's freedom, or by disrupting the moral order of the universe. For God to do the first would rob humanity of all meaning and achievement; and to do the latter would change the cosmos into chaos. It is thus that both Judaism and Christianity have always regarded war as a kind of judgment upon man, and calamity as a vindication of the moral structure and orderliness of the universe.

Man, not God, must prevent war. Man must abolish man's inhumanity to man.

However, God is in the struggle with man to aid and to guide him by His spirit of love and good will. Although He lets man choose the way he will go, He is always struggling along with man throwing His weight for good. Disobedience to God and the laws of life bring evil and strife and suffering. Our defeats are God's defeats; our victories are God's victories. Living God's way brings life. Evil can thus be defeated. "Though the cause of Evil prospers, yet 'tis Truth alone is strong."

SECTION VII

EASTER AND THE ETERNAL LIFE

VII. EASTER AND THE ETERNAL LIFE

1. Passing the Torch
2. The Terrible Meek
3. Life Is Eternal (I)
4. Life Is Eternal (II)
5. The Open Door
6. The Conspiracy of Silence

1. PASSING THE TORCH

One Easter eve several years ago, I, together with some other American friends, was the guest of the Eastern Orthodox Archbishop, or Metropolitan as he was called, at his home in Smyrna. After dinner, he led us to the second-floor balcony of his home overlooking the Metropolitan Churchyard. From there we were to witness the ceremony of the passing of the Light. Ten thousand people had gathered in the churchyard to take part in this ceremony.

Presently the Metropolitan came into the churchyard and approached an open-air altar. He conducted an altar service. Then he took a taper candle, lighted it from the Sacred Flame in the Censer, and passed the flame to the candles of the priests who were standing about the altar. These in turn passed the flame on to others. Thus, the flame on the altar was passed on from hand to hand. It multiplied in waves from the altar until it had flooded every corner of darkness in the great churchyard. What had been, but a few minutes before, a dark mass of humanity was now transformed into a rippling sea of flames. Each candle was minute in itself, but now the thousands illuminated the darkness. Ten thousand hands had passed the torch. Ten thousand souls had received the light.

What a thrilling symbolism this was to those of us who stood on the balcony! Here we stood, as it were, on the threshold of the Eastern Church. This was where the gospel of Jesus had started. This is how it spread. To the utmost parts of the earth it had gone. Jesus had passed on the light to his disciples; these had passed it on to others about them, and so on until the gospel of Jesus had been carried around the world.

That night as we stood there, almost overawed by this impressive service, we could see here and there patches of darkness. Someone had failed to pass the torch. Someone had failed to receive the light. Just as on this night there were patches of darkness in the churchyard below, so today in the world, in continents, in nations, and in communities there are places of darkness because someone has failed to pass on the Light.

Have you received the light? Have you whose life has been filled with the benefits of the light—you who have taken upon yourself His way of life—have you passed the torch? Each preceding generation has borne on the light to us who must take up the torch and sound aloft the cry:

> "To you with failing hands we throw
> The torch: be yours to hold it high."
> Shall we break faith with those who die?

"Let your light so shine before men, that they may see your good works and give glory to your Father who is in heaven."

2. THE TERRIBLE MEEK

Shortly after World War I, Charles Rand Kennedy wrote a most impressive one-act play: "The Terrible Meek." No one can read this play without a feeling of deep anguish. Yet, that anguish changes into hope, hope that the meek shall possess the earth.

The play portrays a British mother kneeling and weeping, awaiting the body of her son who has just been court-martialed and executed. The British Captain, who, with his soldiers, had carried out the execution, is standing by her confessing with shame what they are doing—destroying, killing, murdering—and the reasons why her son had to be executed.

As the play progresses, one begins to wonder, is this mother in reality the Mother of Jesus, and the army Captain, standing there in the shadow of the execution, the Roman Centurian in charge of the crucifixion.

The mother asks the Captain why her dear son whom she has nurtured through childhood into splendid, noble young manhood—why did her son have to die? Why all this destruction, killing and death?

The Captain, feeling shame and moved in pity bursts forth: "They want money. They want power. They want possessions. They want to possess the earth."

And the mother, thinking of her executed son, replies: "And they have won. They have it."

"Have they?" the Captain answers in a flash of insight, "Not while your son hangs there; the meek, the terrible meek; they shall inherit the earth."

So, we go blindly, blunderingly on, not taking time for careful and critical reasoning. We go on building our kingdoms—"kingdoms of this world" on things that have not, cannot endure. We stretch out our hands graspingly to possess the earth. Prestige, and power, money and markets —these are the things we want; but what we get is the enslaved hatreds of struggling peoples, often destruction and death. It can't last; it never has lasted—this building on fear and force. We talk about the security of our possessions. Possessions! If we keep on the way we have been going, we shall not only lose our possessions, we shall lose ourselves, our souls; "for the soul of the earth is man and the love of man," and so often we have brought desolation to both.

Shall we go on seeking security by force? Is America to become the great proponent of the way of force? Is the human story of life on this planet to end in the ignoble self-destruction because men do not have the wit and the wisdom to discover the fallacy of force before it is too late? Perhaps it may be necessary that our present civilization, founded upon force, destroy itself before a just and equitable order can be established. Or perhaps the struggles of our day are but the beginnings of the birth-pangs of a new order which is struggling to be born? Who knows? Only God.

Jesus said: "Blessed (happy—fortunate) are the meek, for they shall inherit the earth."

3. LIFE IS ETERNAL (I)

Easter is the great affirmation of life—life that is real and eternal. When we consider carefully, scientifically the process of life's growth, we see how all life moves up from the material toward the spiritual. Place a tiny seed in the body of the warm earth and it will surge upward, struggling through the various stages of silt and soil, reaching upward until—

> Every clod feels a stir of might,
>   An instinct within which reaches and towers,
> And groping blindly above it for light,
>   Climbs to a soul of grass and flowers.*

And, not content with perfume and beauty, finding still

---

*Vision of Sir Launfal — Lowell.

further development possible through marvelous processes, crowns itself in man. The great creative Power in which men live and have their being "formed man of the dust of the ground." Through creative processes of oxidation, anitosis and metabolism, the materials of earth are transformed into blood, muscle and bone, and transmuted into thought and will and love; and, still pressing on, moves toward life's abiding "house not made by hands but eternal in the heavens."

Can we with certainty carry the process further? What happens to life after material body fails and disintegrates and smolders back into the earth from which it came? Is death "life's greatest adventure?" Does the body return to the earth and the spirit go on to God?

It has not only been the hope, but also the beliefs of the generations of men that life is eternal. Although science can give no definite answer, yet every instinct of human nature, every analysis of human values, and every trend of life's evolutionary processes not only give assurance but also conviction that life is eternal.

> Thou wilt not leave us in the dust;
>> Thou madest man, he knows not why,
>> He thinks he was not made to die;
> And Thou hast made him: Thou art just.

So wrote Alfred Tennyson.

I believe that life is eternal. I cannot prove that it is, but I believe that it is and I hope that it is.

There are many intimations that life is eternal. When I speak of life eternal I mean personal life—your life and my life. It is not that we merge after death with the great ocean of eternity, nor disappear as a conscious being into the vast mass of created life, but that the spirit of each personality lives on. The human spirit expressed in the human personality, I am convinced, is indestructible. It is not a flame which death can smother out. It is not an organism which the grave can disintegrate. Reason repudiates this. If life ends at the grave the universe is irrational, and the God of civilized man is unworthy to be worshipped and loved.

The belief and the desire for eternal life is normal. It persists in the races of men through the ages. It is a trend of the universe and rests upon its integrity. Why not then trust the integrity of the universe of which we are a part to keep faith with this demand of human nature. To do otherwise is irrational; for, if nothing abiding comes out of personality after death, the whole creative process of life becomes meaningless and purposeless. It is impossible to believe that God, the power in which we live, would bring the human spirit up to such significance and then let it perish into nothingness. Rather we hold to what George Herbert Palmer wrote about his wife, Alice Freeman Palmer, when she died: "Though no regrets are proper for the manner of her death, who can contemplate the face of it and not call the world irrational if, out of deference to a few particles of disordered matter, it excludes so fair a spirit." All reasoning men believe,

> Not one good shall be destroyed
> Or cast as rubbish to the void,
> When God has made the pile complete.

This is central in Christianity. Eternal life is the theme of all Christian teaching. Christianity is concerned more with life than just with immortality. Jesus' whole teaching was about life—life, real, eternal. The great word of Christianity is "life," not "death," nor even "soul." While immortality suggests deathlessness, resurrection, as expressed in the New Testament emphatically affirms the re-creation of man through death.

Recall the words of Jesus: "Unless a grain of wheat falls into the ground and dies, it remains alone; but if it dies, it bears much fruit. He who loves his life loses it, and he who hates his life in this world will keep it for eternal life." (John 12: 24, 25) Dying to live—this is central in Christianity. The whole process of nature reveals this fact. In dying, the seed lives. So, in dying, man lives. This is a law of life.

"This is life eternal," said Jesus, "that they may know Thee, the only true God and Jesus Christ whom Thou hast sent." (John 17:3) And when he hung dying on the cross he assured the penitent thief, "This day you will be with me in paradise." Jesus' disciples soon realized that "God raised him up, having loosed the pangs of death, because it was not possible for him to be held by it." (Acts 2:24) They knew that Jesus had built into his life that which death could not destroy. We, too, can build into our life that which death can never destroy if, like Jesus, we live the spirit of God in life.

4. LIFE IS ETERNAL (II)

Christianity has refused to think that the earthly life of man—brief, broken, troubled—is meaningless, without hope and without enduring worth, and that it melts away into oblivion and nothingness.

True, our fathers—and some of our contemporaries—have had some crude notions about the "hereafter." They have formed fantastic descriptions of heaven and hell. Yet amid this quest for meaning, they never surrendered the belief that this life is involved in a higher purpose which determines life's true character and destiny. This belief has enriched life. It caused our fathers to live more reasonable lives; and, furthermore, it made many of them willing to lay down their life rather than lose the freedom and dignity with which God had endowed life. They understood better than we, even though we are threatened with nuclear annihilation, that each man must die. Thus, while confronting the reality and inevitability of death, life, not death, became the deep concern of their existence.

To an earlier generation the "ultimate concern," of which Paul Tillich has written, was expressed in other worldliness. Now in this year of our Lord, the concern has swung too far in the opposite direction. We judge everything, even Jesus' gospel of eternal life, by its immediate usefulness in promoting our earthly welfare, with the result that the sense of eternity dwindles away, and death seems the ultimate disaster.

Too often the resurrection of Jesus is thought of as a miracle, as an interruption of the law-abiding order of our universe caused by God's concern to vindicate His son who "was obedient unto death." Accepting this belief takes away the possibility that the resurrection can have meaning for God's other children, including you and me. The teachings of the New Testament set forth a more meaningful view. It gives validity to the faith that not only is Jesus, the Christ, risen from death into life that is eternal, but also we are risen with him. The biblical description of death is that it is not only a natural event at the close of earthly life; but, more importantly, it is a process which lies within the order of our universe and touches all humanity.

The Christian faith is relevant to the needs of man in this life. But it does not stop with the here and now. It is the touch of eternity found in the teachings, the life and the spirit of Jesus which helps men grasp the meaning of life and to bear with faith and fortitude the vicissitudes confronted in the quest for life that is real, abundant and eternal.

That we should pass through death into life is not incredible. The thing that is incredible is life, your life, my life, all life. The most marvelous, unfathomable thing is life. Whence life? Whence this mysterious universe, the sun and moon and stars? Whence this green, this beautiful, this good earth? These are realities! Life is real! Some Power has called it out of the yet unknown. This Power we call God has, through His marvelous creativity, called the worlds into being. What a marvelous process! "Except a grain of wheat fall into the earth and die it remains alone," said Jesus; "but if it dies it bears much fruit." "We do not believe in immortality because we can prove it, but we try to prove it because we cannot help believing it." So said James Martineau with penetrating insight.

Jesus, who "tasted death for every man," has made death the gateway into eternal life for every man. In his way, in his spirit, life is eternal. "I am the resurrection and the life," said Jesus, "He who believes in me, though he die, yet shall he live, and whoever lives and believes in me shall never die."

It is in this hope that we can look forward to the ongoing life that is eternal.

5. THE OPEN DOOR*

"I know that my Redeemer liveth! And because he lives I too, I too, shall live!" Thus ends a deeply inspirational Easter solo based on Job's triumphant affirmation of faith in eternal life.

The message of Easter is not seasonal. It is eternal. "For God so loved the world that He gave His only begotten son, that whosoever believeth in him shall not perish, but have everlasting life." Abundant life! Eternal, now, continuing! What a priceless gift, impossible of comprehension. A way of life which challenges the finest potential. A way of life which conquers death.

---

*Written by Azora Reese Mathews

The message of Easter is a message of renewal. Then how shall we meet the crisis in life which we call death?

Shortly after a very dear one went on ahead a young electrician came to the house to service some equipment. With concern he expressed his sympathy to me. "But this is a part of life," I replied. With relief he said, "I am so glad to hear you say that. In my work, careful as I may be, I realize that some day I may touch that hot wire. My wife and I have discussed this, have talked with our minister, and have an understanding. We believe that life is continuing, that should this happen I would never be far away. I would want her to remarry and be happy—just to recall once in awhile some of the happy times we had together."

Recently a friend said, "I think I'm a Christian, I believe in God. But I don't think I'll ever see my husband again. We never discussed it. We had no way of knowing really, and I couldn't bear to talk about it." Thus she had failed to take out "insurance protection" against that time. When it is too late the tortuous doubts and longings assail.

We do not know the answers to this greatest of all mysteries. We do know that God is all Goodness and Love. Jesus discussed the next phase of life with his disciples. He assured them, "If it were not so, would I have told you that I go to prepare a place for you?"

Some of the vocabulary surrounding this "renewal of life" may be an obstacle to our thinking. For many the word "death" has connotations of dread finality. Then eliminate it. Death is but a transition.

When a loved one goes on ahead we too often are overwhelmed by a feeling of loss and of separation by some insurmountable barrier which cannot be scaled. Paul asked the question and triumphantly answered it: "Who shall separate us from the love of Christ?" Who shall separate us from the love of those dear to us? Is it not more in keeping with a Master Plan of a loving heavenly Father that we be inseparable? Surely in this vast universe of which we are a part, we are surrounded by "a great cloud of witnesses." Are we not the ones who tend to tune them out rather than tune them in? The door was not closed between Jesus and his disciples, as was evident in their numerous psychic experiences.

Grief is incompatible with the Great Promotion to expanded opportunities in the new phase of life. Loneliness, yes. But by practicing the presence of God within us we can convert loneliness into spiritual dividends for helping others.

It is possible through the elimination of archaic thinking to experience a well-spring of joy within. When there is a background of love and trust in God's goodness and love, to sit with a loved one as he begins that mysterious, exciting journey into the Great Adventure can be an uplifting experience, not a devastating one.

One of Peter Marshall's sermons in *Mr. Jones, Meet the Master* ends with these words:

> Let us, therefore, act like believers,
>   live like Christians so that we can die
>   like Christians—with songs and rejoicing.
> For those we love are with the Lord, we believe,
>   and the Lord has promised to be with us:
>   "Behold I am with you always."
> Well, if they are with Him, and He is with us—
>   THEY CANNOT BE FAR AWAY.

6. THE CONSPIRACY OF SILENCE

Recently a good friend chided me, a minister, in a friendly sort of way, because we ministers generally do not prepare men and women, young and old, to meet realistically the emergencies arising at the time of death. Thus when death comes to one near and dear, those left behind are suddenly confronted with carrying out things at a time when, through grief, one is emotionally least able to act wisely.

The criticism is just and true. I must confess that I, through my ministry, have been remiss in helping people to be prepared for the emergencies arising at the time of a death should it come soon or late, for come it will inevitably to everyone.

As ministers we have counseled those who come to us about everything in life—about marriage, morality, right and wrong, worship, prayer; but seldom do we counsel about making plans for the inevitable departure on "life's greatest adventure." How much more wisdom we should show, and what a helpful service we could render if we would impress upon men and women, young and old, to plan realistically for the time of death as they plan for their home, their children and their education. Thus whether death comes early or in the sunset years, the one left could carry out the plans and desires which had been formulated realistically. Why shouldn't we ministers help our parishioners in this important matter of death as well as of life?

By way of an analogy, if a friend is leaving on a trip abroad, we will talk endlessly about his plans, the places he will visit, art galleries, palaces, hotels, restaurants and the ways of the people in the countries to be visited. But if a friend is about to set out on "life's greatest adventure" we have nothing to say.

Why this conspiracy of silence? Is it because it is considered gloomy and morbid to talk about death? Is it because of a forlorn hope? Why do we hesitate? Is it really because people generally have a basic unbelief in what lies beyond the inevitable and universal incident of death? It might be surprising if it were known how many people hold to a faith in God and in Jesus and in love as a way of life, yet find difficulty in holding a faith in life beyond death.

This wavering faith is no doubt due to the great mystery of death. But someone has reminded us that it should be no more difficult to believe that life will go on than to understand how it began. As to the mystery of the details of life after death, that is what makes it life's greatest adventure. Everything in our universe, the very trend of the universe, indicates that the great creative Power, God, has so designed things that, whatever may happen, life will go on.

Jesus was not reticent about speaking of his approaching death when he shared his last supper with his disciples. Also recall his transforming spiritual experience on the mountaintop with Peter, James and John when he talked in that psychic experience with Moses and Elijah. What do you suppose they were talking about? According to the record we surmise that they were talking about Jesus' death which was to come in Jerusalem; and Jesus continued this talk as he and his three disciples went down the mountainside. Why not? If one has lived in keeping with the spirit of God, if one has lived the eternal life now here on earth, what difference could death make?

So let us have done with the conspiracy of silence. This minister, remembering the wise and just criticism of a friend, now advises you, young couples as well as older, to sit down with the one nearest and dearest to you and shape up the plans for your departure into Life. This is wise and realistic. It is a most helpful and loving service to those who may survive you and love you.

SECTION VIII

FAITH

VIII. FAITH

1. An Enduring Faith
2. An Unconquerable Faith
3. Faith Sets the Course of History
4. Something Magnificent
5. The Trend of the Universe
6. Holding to Our Integrity

1. AN ENDURING FAITH

Can one hold faith in tragic days like these
When war flames forth and men go mad with hate,
When violence and terror seize the state,
And pale religion utters hopeless pleas?
The fearful peoples grovel on their knees.
To arms! They rise; their sons they consecrate
To "noble" death—a sacrifice of fate;
Their Caesar stands and utters stern decrees.
Can one hold faith? The dark years answer no.
What can avail when reason goes astray,
When every man holds any man a foe?
But time is long and kings have feet of clay.
Who rules by hate shall from his throne be hurled.
Lift up your hearts! God has not left his world.

These words were written by my good friend and poet,
the late Thomas Curtis Clark.

James Anthony Froude in his book, *The Science of
History*, wrote, "One lesson, only one, history may be said
to repeat with distinctiveness: That the world is built somehow on moral foundations, that, in the long run, it is well
with the good; it is not well with evil."

Faith in the righteousness of the eternal God may at
times to some seem futile. But, "behind the dim un-

111

known, standeth God within the shadow, keeping watch above his own." An enduring faith may be achieved through the cultivation of a confidence in the goodness and righteousness of God. Righteousness, justice, equity, mercy, good will, love are the spiritual foundations upon which the life of men and nations endure.

It is because of these eternal principles of righteousness which triumph in history and life, that men of faith and vision and courage have been able to find solid rock on which to stand. This is why the poets have sung their sweetest song in dark days. It was out of the dense darkness and exile that Dante wrote his *Divine Comedy*; that Milton out of his blindness wrote his *Paradise Regained*. It was in the winter of discontent that Tennyson wrote *In Memoriam*, that Browning, out of his great sense of loss of loving companionship, wrote his great poems which have touched the hearts of all people. The lofty Hebrew poetry contained in the Psalms came out of the period of exile. With betrayal and Gethsemane and Calvary but a few hours ahead, Jesus led his disciples in a hymn of praise.

It will not matter so much if the material things which we have and hold are swept away from us if we can possess our souls in patience and faith, and live our life in righteousness and come through our days with clean hands, a pure heart, an enduring faith, a sure hope, and an undying love. In order to achieve this we must cultivate the spirit of Jesus in our life. He harmonized his life with the creative Spirit of the universe, God. In his last hour, when all might have seemed to be lost, he could say, "Father, into thy hands I commit my spirit." This is the achievement of a faith that can endure. Through this faith comes a peace which passes all understanding.

A Prayer:　　Give me a faith,
　　　　　　　That I may lift my head
　　　　　　　Above this tangled web.

Give me hope,
That I may see beyond
This mortal realm.

Give me charity,
That I may not condemn
Another's groping search.

2. AN UNCONQUERABLE FAITH

"Thy faith hath made thee whole," said Jesus to a woman whom he had helped. Faith can become a sustaining power in our life. Our Bible is replete with the stories of the accomplishments of men and women of faith. Read Hebrews 11, the roll call of the great heroes of faith, men "who through faith conquered kingdoms, enforced justice, received promises, stopped the mouths of lions, quenched raging fire, escaped the edge of the sword, won strength out of weakness . . . ."

The Psalmist could sing: "Even though I walk through the valley of the shadow of death, I will fear no evil; for thou art with me." The great prophet, Isaiah, wrote, "Have you not known? Have you not heard? The Lord is the everlasting God, the Creator of the ends of the earth. He does not grow faint or grow weary, his understanding is unsearchable. He gives power to the faint, and to him who has no might he increases strength." The Apostle Paul reminded us, "eye hath not seen nor ear heard nor the heart of man conceived what God hath prepared for those who love him." John Greenleaf Whittier, in a dark period, expressed his faith in these words:

Within the maddening maze of things,
And tossed by storm and flood,
To one fixed trust my spirit clings;
I know that God is good.

Faith thus expressed does not mean that we are to submit blindly to fate, nor even to hold to a "courage born of despair"; rather, it is a faith sustained in a hope and trust in "a power not our own which makes for righteousness." It is a faith born out of the great central and universal traditions of human experience, founded upon moral and spiritual values, interpreted by heroic prophets, and made creative by the matchless love of the cross.

The great portrayal of this faith is found in Job of the Old Testament and in Jesus of the New Testament.

The Book of Job gives us a sustaining challenge. This book is the great masterpiece of faith. Job was a good man with an unconquerable faith. The writer of the book portrays God as saying of him, "There is none like him in all the earth, a perfect and an upright man, one that feareth God, and escheweth evil." Yet how severely his faith was tested.

Job had been rich with land, cattle and servants; yet, he was left penniless. Everything, through a series of disasters, was swept away. Even his sons and daughters were destroyed. Amid these tragic losses and in his dejection, he could still say: "The Lord gave, and the Lord taketh away; blessed be the name of the Lord." "In all this," it is recorded, "Job did not sin or charge God with wrong."

There was yet more suffering. Job became afflicted "with loathsome sores from the sole of his foot to the crown of his head." His wife, stunned by all this calamity, admonished him: "Do you still hold fast to your integrity? Curse God, and die." Three of his friends, when they heard of all that had befallen him, came to console and comfort him. But, as it turned out, they were miserable comforters. When they learned how strongly he held to his integrity, and of his unchanging faith in the righteousness of the unsearchable ways of God, they bewail him

and, in the end denounce him as a pretender to righteousness and a hypocrite. They leave him alone in his pain.
Yet he said to them, "Though he slay me, yet will I trust
in him."

Job, once rich, now penniless, his family destroyed,
grievously afflicted, denounced by his friends, apparently
forsaken by God; yet he holds to God his Redeemer.

No other book in the literature of mankind gives such
an aching loneliness of the soul as does this book of Job.
Job made his appeal to the greatness, the wisdom and the
righteousness of God. His faith in God is unconquerable.
Neither will he let his integrity depart from him. In spite
of all, he lifts up his voice in that classic affirmation of
faith: "I know that my redeemer lives, and at last he will
stand on earth; and after my skin has been destroyed, then
without my flesh I shall see God."

What a challenge to our faith! It is easy to hold faith
when everything is fine with us; but faith in times of failure, discouragement and defeat—this is the test. "Until
I die," said Job, "I will not remove my integrity from
me." Here is Job's strength to stand; "Though he slay me,
yet will I trust in him."   If he cannot understand the
marvelous and unsearchable ways of God, he will still
hold to the best within him—his integrity. As Shakespeare
puts it:

> This above all; to thine own self be true,
> And it must follow, as night the day,
> Thou cans't not be false to any man.

Jesus' faith in God is eternal.   His whole life is the
greatest and most inspiring expression of faith in the
annals of men.   But it is in his last night that we see the
ultimate of faith in God. In the Garden of Gethsemane,
when he realized that the end was near, he wanted to live.
He prayed most passionately, "My Father, if it be possible,

let this cup pass from me; nevertheless, not as I will but as thou wilt." Yet in utter confidence he accepted what he knew to be the will of God. He went to the cross. With undying faith in God, as his body gave up his spirit, he prayed, "Father, into thy hands I commit my spirit." In utter confidence, in eternal faith he could commit his all to God.

We, too, can hold to our integrity; we can be true to the best, the highest within us; and having done this, we can leave the rest to God.

3. FAITH SETS THE COURSE OF HISTORY

The lack of faith is one of the greatest, if not the greatest hindrance to human progress in every phase of life. Fear consumes faith. Have you ever compiled a list of our fears? We fear disease, hunger, want, loneliness; we fear Communism and Fascism; we fear atomic power, nuclear bombs—these and a host of other fears. Our life is full of fears. Just how fearful can a people permit themselves to become!

We need faith in ourselves, in our fellowmen and in God.

Jesus, with a deep discernment of life, was continually warning the people of his day against their fears and their anxieties and their lack of faith. "O men of little faith," he would say, "why are you anxious about food and clothing? Your Heavenly Father knows you need these." "Why are you afraid?" "Have faith in God," he was constantly urging. "If you have faith as a grain of mustard seed, you say to this mountain, 'Move hence to yonder place,' and it will move; and nothing will be impossible to you." When he was asked about a most difficult problem, he said, "With men it is impossible, but with God all things are possible." (Matt. 19:25-26)

We are hindered by fears because we have tried to solve our many problems within the framework of our human frailties. We have trusted man's wisdom disregarding the wisdom and the way of the spirit of God. Man's wisdom often violates the moral structure of the universe. So great is man's indifference to the way of God that it seems naive for a minister to remind ourselves that "with man it is impossible, but with God (working with God in harmony with the moral and spiritual structure of the universe) all things are possible."

Only with God will man achieve. "But," the question comes, "how can we get enough people to believe this?" Well, we had better!

In this connection I would like to bring to your attention the conviction of one of our most thoughtful and careful historians, the late Arnold Toynbee. At mid-century a group of American writers, in an interview with Toynbee, asked what kind of a world we might have in the next fifty years.

Arnold Toynbee, out of his keen perception of history, replied: "I do not know what kind of a world we shall have in the next fifty years, but I do know what will make it. It depends upon what men believe. Great multitudes change the course of history for a few decades. Great minds change it for a century or so. But it is great spirits, great believers who, in the long run, set the course of history. Right now man is making up his mind about what he believes. He may decide that he believes in himself—as most Americans do—in which case we shall have chaos. He may decide that he believes in collective humanity—as the Russians do—in which case we shall have slavery. He may decide that he believes in God, the Father of Jesus Christ, in which case the fondest dreams of the race will fall far short of the actual world we can have in the future."

In times like these, one is moved to wonder: Do enough people have enough faith in God?

If we can hold to a faith in the power of the eternal God, especially the faith expressed in the life, the spirit and the way of Jesus, we shall yet achieve. "Truly, truly, I say to you," said Jesus, "he who believes in me will do the works that I do; and greater works than these will he do." (John 14:12)

"With man it is impossible, but with God all things are possible."

4. SOMETHING MAGNIFICENT

Unprecedented changes have been taking place in our world within the past two and one half decades, changes which are profoundly reshaping man's mores, his psychology and his way of life. The release of atomic energy, the development of electronics, and the ever increasing advancement of technology open up a whole new area of hitherto latent power with almost terrifying potentialities which indicate, for the future, changes of even greater magnitude. Sinister forces are bidding for the control of these powers.

When we think of what could happen should such forces ever get control, we can easily permit ourselves to be seized by such fear as will prevent us from bringing our minds to a solution of the problems which must be solved if we are to dwell in security and peace. Rather, we must so strengthen our moral standards and spiritual vision that these powers will always remain under the control of men of wisdom and good will. Along with a high morality and a deep spiritual vision, we must so strengthen our faith in God that we shall follow more closely His way of life for men; for the ultimate triumph lies with men of

good will, with men of high morality, a greater spiritu-
ality and an undaunted faith.

A close study of history confirms this. If we can hold
to a way of faith in the eternal God, especially a faith as
revealed in the life, the way and the spirit of Jesus, we shall
achieve life. Note carefully how one historian stated his
faith.

The late Charles A. Beard, for many years the distinguished professor of history in Columbia University,
writes: "As I look over the drama of history, I find amid
the apparent chaos, evidence of law and plan and immense
achievement of the human spirit, in spite of disaster. I am
convinced that the world is not a mere bog in which men
and women trample themselves in the mire and die. Something magnificent is taking place here amid the cruelties
and tragedies and the supreme challenge to intelligence is
to make the noblest and best in our curious heritage to
triumph and prevail."

Yes, "something magnificent" is taking place in our
world. Men of good will in every walk of life must strive
earnestly to align themselves with the creative process
which is evident wherever and whenever men and women
rise intelligently to work for the common good.

Let us rise to see beyond the sinister forces, the frustrating fears and the baffling tragedies which so often
darken and discourage our life. Let us look intelligently to
see and understand the magnificent power that binds the
Pleiades to their course, that holds the cords of Orion,
that guides the trackless winds, that gives the day for work
and the night for rest, that makes the rose to bloom and
the stars to shine, that releases the energy from the materials of the earth, and, above all, that places the upward
reach of thought and self-consciousness and will and love
in the hearts of men and women.

5. THE TREND OF THE UNIVERSE

"I doubt not thro all ages one increasing purpose runs." So wrote Alfred Tennyson. To this we would link, "There is a power, not ourselves, that makes for righteousness."

Jesus had much to say about the power and love of God. The Apostle Paul warned the people of his day not to let their faith "rest in the wisdom of men, but in the power of God." Christians hold that God is the creative power back of the universe, that "binds the sweet influence of the Pleiades, or looses the bands of Orion," that "has made from one every nation of men to live on the face of the earth," and that "in him we live and move and have our being."

There is this creative moral, ethical and spiritual power in the universe that makes for order and righteousness. This power works unceasingly against disorder and evil. It moves to defeat all who oppose mercy and equity, liberty and freedom, justice and love. History teaches us—if we have the wisdom to learn—that this power has decreed that right is greater than might, that the way of love is better than the way of hate. Yes, the power of love can exceed the power of the atom.

Down across three thousand years of history there comes to us the story of Sisera. Sisera was a ruthless warrior who was threatening the life of early Israel. No man of Israel had the courage to go out to defend Israel against Sisera's chariots and multitudes. It remained for a woman, Deborah by name, to lead the defense of Israel. She and her army stood courageously at the river Kishon and defeated Sisera and the mighty forces with him. The record of this battle states: "The stars in their courses fought against Sisera." (Judges 4:5)

Tyrants and men deluded by the lust for power still try to fight against the stars, but they go down in defeat. This is history. Those who go against the power of the universe, those who disregard the God-given rights of others have left nothing to humanity but destruction and death; they and those who follow them leave behind them a trail of bones, ashes and death. The power that sustains the stars in their courses goes against the tyrants.

In all historical writing there is no finer illustration of this truth that there is a sustaining power that works unceasingly against evil and for righteousness than that found in Victor Hugo's comment on the Battle of Waterloo. Hugo writes: "Was it possible for Napoleon to win the battle? No. Why? Not on account of Wellington, and not on account of Blucher, but on account of God. Bonaparte a victor at Waterloo did not harmonize with the law of the universe which was preparing an order in which Napoleon had no place.... The moment had arrived for the Incorruptible Supreme Equity of the universe to act. The principles on which depend the regular gravitations of the moral order had complained. Streaming blood, over-crowded graveyards, and mother's tears are the pleaders that stir Infinity. When earth suffers from excessive burdens, Infinity hears her groans. It was in Infinitude that Napoleon had been denounced and his fall decreed. Waterloo was not a battle; it was a trend of the universe."

Our realization and understanding of this trend of the universe increases as our wisdom and our understanding of history increases. So also we must come to realize that this trend, motivated by the Power that holds an astronaut in his journey into space, that binds the planets in their courses, that places limits on the restless seas, holds our life, too, within its mighty and gracious keeping.

6. HOLDING TO OUR INTEGRITY

In the immortal Biblical drama of Job there is much for us as individuals and as a people. When Job is driven almost beyond endurance by pain, by desertion of his friends, and by the incomprehensible mysteries of his Creator, he cries out, "I will not remove my integrity from me." When there seems to be nothing left to sustain, we can hold to our integrity, to the best that is in us.

There is an eternal goodness in the universe. There is a moral order in the universe. There is integrity in the universe. This universe is friendly. Many can affirm with Immanuel Kant, that, "Two things fill my soul with always new and increasing wonder and awe, and often persistently my thought busies itself therewith: the starry heaven above me and the moral law within me." These are a part of our consciousness of existence.

The moral order of our universe is such that "truth crushed to earth will rise again." Truth may be ignored, it may be circumvented, it may be temporarily thwarted; but there is no defeat for truth. It is most regrettable when men in positions of power pervert truth. When people fail to hold to their integrity, they lose their credibility, their influence and their power. When people hold to their integrity, they achieve personal character and the confidence of their fellows. They rise above defeat to personal triumph.

Abraham Lincoln, when an obscure congressman from Illinois, voted against the Mexican War. Many said that he was headed for political obscurity. But he did what he thought was right. "He would rather be right than President." He became one of our most honored Presidents. Gandhi went to jail in India rather than give up in a cause which he felt was right and just. He held to his integrity. He brought independence to a sub-continent of people.

Jesus went to the cross to bear witness to God, and today multitudes follow him and acclaim him as their Lord and Master.

Nations, too, must hold to their integrity. America stands today at the judgment bar. It is the judgment bar of God. Other nations have stood before the judgment of God. Many of them have been weighed in the balance and found wanting. Will America hold to her integrity? Will she bear witness to truth? Let her not seek her stability and honor in acquiescence to falsehood and compromise of truth; not in the vain promises of clemency for immoral, unethical and illegal acts against the public trust; nor in the seductive, pleading voices that promise all sorts of favors in order to save face; nor in the cruel smolderings of false liberty promised by political chicanery. America will not find honor or inspiration for the future here. Rather, she will find it in the measureless sweep of the spirit's vision, in a commitment to integrity, character and the abiding value of truth.

It is deeply regrettable when men in high official positions in government will betray the nation's trust because of the lack of personal integrity. Yet far more serious and deplorable is the moral apathy on the part of many Americans as expressed in their passing over so lightly the illegal acts, the betrayal of public trust, the disregard for truth, and the excusing of scandalous acts as "politics as usual," and as just a "deplorable incident." All this should reveal to every thoughtful person the level to which morality can fall in a nation's life.

We must examine continually the moral life of our country. We are living in an orderly, law abiding universe, a universe of moral laws as well as physical laws. We cannot break these laws; we can only break ourselves against them. We can defy them, but "the soul that sinneth shall surely die." "The mills of God grind slowly, but they grind exceedingly fine."

We are being judged by other nations. But more, we are being judged by the eternal Power back of the universe— God. The time has come to realize the dreams of a nation founded upon moral integrity and abiding values. Never before in human history have men had the knowledge to discern wisdom and truth as they now possess. Never, since Jesus, have men been able to understand more clearly what is the will and the way of God. Can they achieve the character and the will to realize it?

Christians cannot and must not disassociate themselves from the difficulties and confusions which confront men and nations. We can never be at ease until we have faced the highest demands which life makes upon us, until we have acknowledged our responsibility to God for the life of our time. "The truth of the Lord endureth forever."

> Who will live to slay the false?
> Who will die to prove the true?
> Who will claim the earth for God?
> Who will build the world anew?

—Thomas Curtis Clark

SECTION IX

GOD

IX. GOD

1. God in the Universe
2. The Will of God
3. Getting Through to God
4. How God Speaks to Us
5. God or Government
6. God's Dreams
7. Can Man by Searching Find God?

1. GOD IN THE UNIVERSE

When I look into the starry heavens at night and behold the moon, the planets and the myriad of stars, I must admit that the universe is! I am moved to exclaim; "O God, how great Thou art!" For, since there is this creation which we can see, surely there is a Creator.

The infinite expanse of the universe, its growth through the immeasurable eons of time, the boundless range of its change, and the rational orderliness which prevails, all demand infinite Intelligence which motivates it. Awe-inspiring as is the timelessness and the spacelessness of the universe to the scientist, the most marvelous part of the universe is its orderliness. Everything moves in precise order according to laws.

As I walk out into the yard which surrounds the house in which we live, I am, if thoroughly appreciative, aware and at times overwhelmed by the living, purposeful and beautiful universe about me. The green grass beneath, the trees with branches reaching upward, and the beautiful flowers are all vibrant with life and meaning.

As I behold the ebb and flow of the tides, the phases of the moon, the coming of winter and of spring not far behind, the never-failing break of each day in its mistive dawning and its inevitable close often in a blaze of golden sunset, if I am thoughtful and understanding, I acknowledge that the orderly mystery of the universe and its life-giving energy and the gracious purpose of its Creator are shrouded in vast wonder until we learn that all law supposes a law-giver and all energy and all life has its source.

The Universe expresses God. Modern science, far from doing away with God, gives a more realistic and more profound conception of God. Arthur H. Compton once stated: "I believe that the very existence of the amazing world of the atom points to a purposeful creation, to the idea that there is a God and an intelligent purpose back of everything." Our expanding knowledge of the universe is replacing our long-held childish conception of God and His creation.

One of the most serious handicaps under which religion moves in our scientific age is the fact that so many religious people cherish their childhood conception of God as the changeless and ultimate norm by which they test the existence of God. People grow up, but their idea of God does not grow in this dynamic, atomic and space age. Their other ideas grow, so also should their knowledge and understanding of God continue to grow.

As our knowledge of the universe grows, the Power motivating the universe is expressed more clearly. In an infinite variety of ways God is revealed to those who will open up their mind and life to Him. Communication with the infinite is determined not by the audibility of God's voice, but by our capacity and our willingness to hear. He speaks through His universe. As Emerson has stated it, "Nature is too thin a screen; the glory of the omnipotent God bursts through."

> I raised my eye aloft, and I beheld
> The scattered chapters of the universe
> Gathered and bound in a single book
> By the austere and tender hand of God.
> —*Dante*

2. THE WILL OF GOD

The will of God is a phrase we often use, but we use it carelessly. Just what is the will of God? Often, when I have tried to minister to people in sorrow over the loss of a loved one, and, as I have heard them say, "It is the will of God and I shall accept it," there comes into my mind a disturbing question: Is it the will of God? How carelessly we use this phrase!

What is the will of God? So many books have been written in an attempt to answer this question that it seems folly even to present it in this short space and most certainly to attempt an answer. Nevertheless, I shall pass on some things which, I believe, may be helpful.

First, I would suggest that you read Leslie Weatherhead's book *The Will of God*. For several years Dr. Weatherhead was the minister of the City Temple in London. In a little book of some fifty pages, he has given his answer—a most helpful answer—to this question.

Secondly, I would suggest that you give careful study to what an early follower of Jesus wrote to the group of Christians in Rome: "Do not be conformed to this world but be transformed by the renewing of your mind, that you may prove what is the will of God, what is good and acceptable and perfect." (Romans 12:2 RSV) As Dr. Goodspeed's translation puts it: "You must not adopt the customs of this world but by your new attitude of mind be transformed so that you can find out what God's will is— what is good, pleasing, and perfect." This "new attitude of mind" was a way of thinking motivated by the spirit of Jesus. As Jesus came to know and understand God, he thought of Him as spirit; and, as he came to understand the will and way of God, he felt God to be the reality, the ultimate truth back of the universe. "To this end," said Jesus, "I was born ... to bear witness to truth," and truth to Jesus was God.

Thus, I submit, to learn more of the will of God, we must let our mind be motivated by the spirit of Jesus; and, as the Apostle Paul wrote to the Christians in Philippi, "Whatever is true, whatever is honorable, whatever is just, whatever is pure, whatever is lovely, whatever is gracious, if there is any excellence, if there is anything worthy of praise, think on these things." (I Phil. 4:8, RSV) Let this way of thinking motivate you in your approach to an understanding of the will of God.

To know God, to gain an understanding of His way in this world of which we are a part must underlie the search of man for all knowledge. Out of this increasing understanding of God will come an increasing understanding of His will. The will of God cannot be expressed in a word nor a phrase. It must be experienced. It is embodied in all that lies back of the work, the wisdom, the creativity, and the spirit of God. Gather up the meaning of all these unto one whole, and we shall approach the meaning of the will of God.

Whatever is creative of life, whatever enhances life, and whatever ennobles life—this is God's will. The beautiful, the true, the pure, the lovely, peace and good will—these are good. They are the expression of God's will. Whatever destroys life, hinders life, exploits life, degrades life—these are evil. Lust, immorality, slander, selfishness, injustice, inequity, murder, war—these are not God's will.

Truly, to the wise, the thoughtful, the concerned who have abstained from all that is evil and who have dedicated themselves to all that is good—to these, who have been willing to seek after God's creative spirit, have the deep mysteries of His will ever been revealed. These will grow in the grace and knowledge of our Lord and Savior, Jesus Christ.

3. GETTING THROUGH TO GOD

Recently, on a Monday morning, I met a friend who said he had been to church the day before and had learned something he had never known before. This was good, I thought, and I was curious to know what my friend had learned. When I asked him, he answered, "I learned that God does not understand English." Now my curiosity was really aroused, for I had always assumed that God understood English, so I further asked my friend how he came by his new knowledge. He explained it this way: he had gone to church on Sunday and heard the preacher give his sermon in English but all his prayers were in Spanish. "Therefore," my friend concluded, "God speaks only in Spanish." I wonder! I was not convinced.

Nevertheless, I was still curious, for I recalled reading in George Bernard Shaw's *Saint Joan* the conversation between the English chaplain and the commanding officer as Joan of Arc was burning at the stake. The chaplain says, "The maid does not tell the truth. The voices she hears are not the voices of God and his angels. Are they not in French? God speaks English!" There is the difficulty! If God were only well enough educated He could speak all the languages of all the great nations! Is this what is wrong in our world? We pray to God; but look at our world filled with strife and the clash of wars between nations, conflict of races, and hatred among men. Cannot God understand?

Perhaps the misunderstanding is not with God. Could it be with us? When we try to get through to God, is it the eternal God to whom we pray?

On this same Sunday, when my friend learned that, "God does not understand English," I heard the preacher in the church where I worshipped that day describe how the Germans on one side of the Rhine and the French on the other side have for generations fought each other in bloody wars, yet they claim to hold to the same God. The Protestants in Germany and the Protestants in France recite the same creed, yet fight each other; the Catholics in Germany and the Catholics in France adhere to the same church, yet fight each other. Both claim to pray to the same God. I wonder!

One is forced to the conclusion that there are nationalist leaders and selfish people; the one group thinks of their national prestige, and the millions on the other side are equally concerned about their national interests. In reality, each nation prays to their own national god, not to the eternal God and Father of mankind. Shall we then conclude that, as history has remarked, God is on the side of the largest armies? Not yet. The important question is not so much whether we get through to God as whether God gets through to us.

According to the Biblical record, God speaks to man in His "mighty acts," through events, through the trends of life in time and space, together with the meanings they carry. Only as discerning minds can see in emerging situations and the outcome of human actions in the moral order as the judgment of God, can the voice of God be heard by man. World War I did not "end war" nor "make the world safe for democracy"; it only created causes for more and greater wars. World War II only crushed one cruel and brutal nationalism to give rise to a much more sinister form which has divided the world in two and filled it with suspicion and hatred and fear of universal annihilation.

We must come to the place where, in the affairs of men and nations, we love our fellow men sincerely. There is no other way to build an abiding civilization than on the basis of the great commandment: "Thou shalt love the Lord your God with all your heart and with all your soul, and with all your mind . . . and your neighbor as yourself."

4. HOW GOD SPEAKS TO US

The story is told that one day in Paris a religious procession carrying a crucifix passed Voltaire and a friend. Voltaire, who was known as an infidel, lifted his hat. "What!" the friend asked, "are you reconciled with God?" To which Voltaire replied, "We salute, but we do not speak."

How aptly that phrase describes the relationship of many modern people with God. They believe that there is God; they find it most difficult to explain the universe without Him, but they maintain no personal relationship with him. They salute, but they do not speak.

This attitude cannot be the Christian attitude toward God. Jesus portrays God as standing at the door of every human life knocking to gain entrance to come in and commune with us. God does not hold himself aloof from man speaking only through certain spokesmen or only through the writings of messengers of long ago. He would speak to all who will listen to the still, small voice of calm and peace. Though He may often speak to us in His "mighty acts" and in the unfolding events of history, in infinitely varying ways He would commune with us. Through the marvels of nature, the good earth and the starry heavens, He speaks to us. Through other forms of language, He speaks. The beauty of the sunset, the rolling thundering clouds, the gentle rain, the "day unto day uttereth speech and night unto night declare the knowledge" of God. The silence is sometimes his voice. He also speaks in defeats or success or unexpected events or a precious friendship or by the life of a little child, as George Eliot reminds us in *Silas Marner*: "In old days there were white-winged angels who came and took men by the hand and led them away from the city of destruction; but we see no white-winged angels now, yet a hand is put in theirs, and the hand may be that of a little child." These and many others are the languages of God to all who will open up their heart and mind to understand God. God's word is a living word to be heard by the soul that is in tune with the infinite. If we will listen, we may catch the accent of the holy Spirit amid life's experiences.

In George Bernard Shaw's *Saint Joan*, when Joan of Arc speaks repeatedly of the "voices" she hears, one of the officers asks, "How do you mean? Voices?" The maid replies, "I hear voices telling me what to do. They come from God."

The weakling King Charles, whom she has helped to have crowned, impatiently exclaims, "Oh your voices, your voices. Why don't the voices come to me? I am king, not you."

Joan answers, "They do come to you; but you do not hear them. You have not sat in the field in the evening listening for them. When the angelus rings you cross yourself and have done with it; but if you prayed with your heart, and listened to the thrilling of the bells in the air after they stop ringing, you would hear the voices as I do."

> Therefore, as the Holy Spirit says,
> "Today, when you hear his voice,
> do not harden your hearts."
> *(Heb. 3:7-8)*

5. GOD OR GOVERNMENT*

Once again our generation is confronted with the age old philosophical and moral issue of loyalty to conscience

---

*This subject is discussed at greater length in the book *The Quest for Life*, by William B. Mathews (Chapter 15), Boston, The Christopher Publishing House.

or government. Our government has long recognized the right of its citizens to dissent. But the issue goes deeper than dissent; it reaches into the moral foundation of life itself: when one's conscience comes into conflict with the government, is one to obey one's conscientious convictions or the law of the nation? Is one to obey God or men? In few generations has this issue been drawn more sharply than our own.

The Vietnam war raised many moral issues in the mind and conscience of not only many Americans but also of the people of other nations. This fundamental and moral issue was drawn dramatically and clearly in our nation's courts with the indictment by the government in Washington of Dr. Benjamin Spock, the world renowned pediatrician, and the Rev. William Sloan Coffin, the then chaplain of Yale University, and three others for their opposition to the Vietnam war. Spock and Coffin and the others admit that they knowingly and willfully are disobeying the law, but they maintain that there is a higher moral law which they choose to follow, regardless of the consequences.

This is the age-old conflict between conscience and government. Far back in the ancient records of men we see it drawn. Jeremiah, in ancient Israel, clearly presents the religious issue of loyalty to God or government. Plato, the Greek philosopher, presents the philosophic issue between conscience and the laws of the state. Socrates dramatizes it in his death. Jesus set it forth clearly, when he said; "No one can serve two masters; for either he will hate the one and love the other, or he will be devoted to the one and despise the other. You cannot serve God and mammon."

The disciples of Jesus faced the issue early. When they were arrested and commanded by the supreme court of their people to cease teaching God's way as revealed by Jesus, they replied; "Whether it be right in the sight of

God to harken unto you rather than unto God, you may judge; for we cannot but speak the things we have seen and heard." The early Christians came into conflict with the Roman Empire because they placed loyalty to Christ above loyalty to Caesar. Many paid for their loyalty with death. In the middle ages Martin Luther chose to hold to his personal convictions against the laws of Church and State in his memorable stand: "Here I stand. I can do nothing else. God help me." When Karl Barth, the present-day theologian, refused to obey the laws of Nazi Germany —as did many other Germans—he said: "What I have to say in this matter is simple—I say no, without reservation or qualification." Martin Neimoeler defied Nazi law and was sent into a concentration camp; Deitrich Bonhoeffer was executed.

In many generations men have had to make their choice of obeying God or man. We find the issue dramatized in Sophocles' classic "Antigone," a drama old yet ever true whose truth can never be dimmed. Antigone rebels against the laws of the state. Her brother had been a traitor to his city and had been put to death. By order of the state his body is to be left unburied as a fitting idignity. But Antigone resolves to give her brother a decent burial. "There is a law of love deeper than the shame of treachery and higher than the laws of the state." She responds to this law. She, too, is condemned to die for her disobedi-ence, and to die by starvation. The governor of the city, her uncle, pleads with her:

"And didst thou dare to disobey these laws?" to which she courageously replied:

"I did not deem thine edicts strong enough
That thou, a mortal man, shouldst overpass
The unwritten laws of God that know no change."

The unwritten, unalterable laws of God that know no

change!   These are the laws which undergird the life of
this universe.   They must underlie the laws of all nations.
The conflict between conscience and government will
continue until men and nations realize this.   If we choose
these laws of God, we have life; if we reject them we have
conflict.   "Behold," comes the verdict of the ages, "I have
set before you life and death. . . Therefore, choose life."

6. GOD'S DREAMS

"We are such stuff as dreams are made of," once wrote
a master poet.   But more, we are "God's Dreams."   Mankind has ever been stretching onward and upward toward
the realms of his dreams.   The ancient prophet, Joel,
declared God as saying,

> I will pour out my spirit on all flesh;
>   your old men shall dream dreams,
>   and your young men shall see visions.

Jesus, too, dreamed his dreams.

He dreamed that every soul on earth
Should worship God . . . .
He dreamed that every earth-born child
Should have its rights: a happy birth,
Love's guiding care through youth's hard years
To manhood's dawn. He dreamed that fears
Should be no part of human fate,
That love should cleanse all hearts of greed and hate.

He dreamed his dream, and wrought as best he knew;
He dreamed, and God will make his dream come true.*

Since we are the dreams of God, our dreams, too—

*Thomas Curtis Clark

however broken or unfulfilled—are something more than the imaginations born of our minds; they are the visions of a brighter dawn beyond the night, a hope of light beyond the shadow, and a faith of love to the end of the world.

What does God dream of man, and man himself dare to dream? That man shall learn to be a brother to his fellows, that greed and cruelty and lust shall pass away, that every busy mart and furrowed field shall become the place where each shall help the other until all shall reach their goal, that man shall cease from hating so that this sad world may realize the age-long dream of his soul.

It seems a dim dream, far off and almost unreal in days like these. But if man can have a dream and a purpose, and a faith which, with love, reaches beyond the horror, the tragedy and agony of war, mankind may yet achieve life that is rich and righteous and eternal. With faith, hope and love—these three—bound together in a supreme commitment to God, mankind can be assured that at long last God's will is done on earth as it is in heaven. With a surrender to the spirit of God we can be assured that despite tragedy there is joy in life; that despite evil there is good. We are not the slaves of evil and death; there is always God. God is life; we are God's dreams.

God lives and reigns and loves; life is longer than time; love is stronger than death; God's truth sets us free eternally!

> "Dreams are they—but they are God's dreams!
> Shall we decry them and scorn them?
> That men shall love one another,
> That white shall call black man brother,
> That greed shall pass from the market place,
> That lust shall yield to love of the race,
> That man shall meet with God face to face—
> Dreams are they all,
>   But shall we despise them—
>   God's Dreams!

Dreams are they—to become man's dreams!
Can we say nay as they claim us?
That men shall cease from their hating,
That war shall soon be abating,
That the glory of kings and lords shall pale
That the pride of dominion and power shall fail,
That the love of humanity shall prevail—
Dreams are they all,
    But shall we despise them—
    God's Dreams!"

—Thomas Curtis Clark

7. CAN MAN BY SEARCHING FIND GOD?

Mankind still utters the age-old cry: "O that I knew where I might find Him." Job also raised the age-old question: "Cans't thou by searching find God?" Can we come to a greater knowledge and understanding of the power in which we "live and move and have our being?" Can we find God? What is God?

God is the Father, the Creative Spirit, the unifying urge expressing Himself in the natural order. He is the loving Son the intelligent good will, the love expressing Himself in the brotherhood of man. He is the creative, the loving, the eternal Spirit expressing Himself in thought, in truth, and in the spiritual values.

Where is God? God is in life, in thought, and in spirit. We find Him expressing Himself in nature, in history, in personality.

Everyone must seek for a concept of God which will aid him to realize God in his life. We should seek to study the most intelligent approaches which can be made through science, philosophy and religion. We must seek to review and to claim for ourselves all that the past has learned out of its struggles in its quest for God. There must be no end to the search. Yet, in the final analysis, each of us must seek to come before the presence of God Himself if we are to know Him. We must penetrate beyond the speculations of philosophy and theology; we must surge beyond the struggles, the questings, the findings of the past; for, let it be clearly recognized, that back of all the philosophical and theological conceptions of God, beyond the present knowledge of God—be this ever so verifiable by the accumulated truth of the centuries of seeking—there stands God, above and beyond all, the same yesterday, today and forever. Yesterday's concepts of God are not quite satisfying to us; today's concepts, let us believe, will not be adequate for our children tomorrow; for the human mind's grasp of God is ever growing.

When in some significant moment, a man comes to stand amid the silence of eternity; when, in his inmost being, he has an awareness of life's eternal values; when, from his mind, he has penetrated beyond the speculations of philosophy and theology; when, in the purity of his heart, he has felt the spirit freed from selfishness and strife, then it is that he comes to stand before God. When he thus stands before God, he realizes how trivial are man's speculations, how insignificant are his conceptions, how frail and fruitless are all his seekings; for, above all, beyond all and in all is God in all His majesty, yet humility; in all his greatness, yet simplicity; in all His power, yet tenderness. Then only can a man see life as it ought to be seen, for he has caught a glimpse of the eternal God. In such a moment he cries out not, "What is God?" but "Such knowledge is too wonderful for me. I cannot attain unto it." God becomes a great spiritual reality so that he asks not "Where is God?" but "Whither shall I go from thy spirit, or whither shall I flee from thy presence?"

Be still and know that I am God,
  Ye who with fret and fears are worn;
Who hear no voice when tempests beat;
  Who faint, by sorrows overborn;
Who dwell in shadows of defeat.

Be still and know that I am God.
                    —*Thomas Curtis Clark*

SECTION X

HUMOR

X. HUMOR

1. The Therapy of Humor
2. The Humor of Jesus

1. THE THERAPY OF HUMOR

Humor is as old as speech. Laughter rings in all tribes and nations of men around the world. And well that it does, for otherwise there might not be any men in the world. There is a therapeutic value in humor.

With more humor there would be no generation gap. This is so well illustrated by the boy who went away to college. He was so glad to get away from home, for his father was so dumb that he hardly knew anything. After the four years in college, following graduation, the young man came home to spend a few days with the "old folks." In these few days at home he was greatly surprised, in fact he was dumbfounded to discover how much his father had learned in the last four years.

Some of us "senior citizens" recently sat in on a discussion between some teenagers and their parents where the give and take was on "the generation gap." We, "senior citizens," had raised families who are now out and on their own filling places of responsibility with great credit. Some of these are M.D.'s, Ph.D.'s and Masters in their arts. Strangely, we did not know that there had been a generation gap. But how could we have known; we were "old folks."

Following the discussion on the so-called generation gap, my wife talked with some of the young people and commended them on their forthright performance. Then she asked, "Do you young people have a sense of humor? Are you able to stand back and take a look at yourself and laugh at yourself? People of every age are guilty of taking themselves too seriously. Changing the perspective and being able to see the humor, the absurd in our situations can resolve differences and relieve tensions." "Oh wad some power the giftie gie us, To see ourselves as others see us."

One of the girls in the group brightened up and getting the point said, "Oh, I think that this is a wonderful idea. I think that is a good philosophy."

Humor is a form of philosophy, for it is a view of life. It is a wholesome, a rewarding, a relaxing way of life. Humor sees beyond the tensions of our differences and grasps the real point at issue. Conflicts are never even-sided, nor wholly one-sided. Humor relaxes and helps us to see this. When things get rough, if one can laugh, one can relax. Humor produces a release for conflict, a resolution of troublesome differences. What kills us is what we cannot laugh off.

When we consider the trivial, the absurd things which often create tensions today—the weather, it's too hot or it's too cold; "the kids get into your hair," the generation gap, married life's "tempest in a tea-pot"—we can see how tensions build up until they explode. It is all right if the explosion is laughter. This may not resolve everything, but a big explosion can resolve quite a lot. The choice is obvious; you can go on and get a heart attack, or you can laugh.

This is not being facetious. Humor is warm, tender, friendly and understanding. Humor and a sense of concern are not incompatible. Humor and seriousness of intent always strengthen each other.

Abraham Lincoln was always adroit in handling serious situations with a masterful use of humor. When some wanted to relieve General Grant of his command because he drank so much whisky, Lincoln was not unconcerned about the situation; but his reply was, "I wish I knew what brand he has, I would supply it to all my generals."

Jesus, too, had a penetrating sense of humor in his teachings.

One of the hardest things which can be said of anyone is, "He has no sense of humor." Humor is one of the redeeming graces of life. It has an exceptional therapeutic value. "Laugh and the world laughs with you, weep and you weep alone."

2. THE HUMOR OF JESUS

Jesus had a real, a delightful sense of humor. Too often Christianity has portrayed Jesus as a gloomy personage. True, he was "a man of sorrows," "acquainted with grief" who took upon himself the burden of all humanity.

Yet, this is not the whole picture of Jesus. He, who was so deeply involved in all humanity, felt and shared the whole of life. It would be unreasonable to conclude that one so rich in emotions and in understanding of his fellows would feel only the tragic and the sorrow in life and never the incongruous and the humorous. No one could have looked through human nature as Jesus looked through it without smiling at its absurdities. Some of his most telling teachings were through the use of humor.

He used grotesque exaggeration effectively. Recall the time when he saw through the hypocrisy of those with a formal view of religion, and related the incident of the busy-body with the beam of lumber in his own eye trying to remove the speck of dust from his neighbor's eye. Or, again, picture the stickler for form straining the gnat out of his cup of wine before drinking only thereafter to swallow a camel.

These and other incidences illustrate the way Jesus could look at the foibles and absurdities of his fellow men;

such as, the little man who, by worrying about it, tries to add a cubit to his stature, and the rich man trying to worm his way into heaven like a camel—hump, long legs and all— trying to squeeze through the eye of a needle. Jesus must have smiled at the bit of comedy in the little wealthy man, Zacchaeus, climbing up into a tree to get a glimpse of Jesus passing by.

Was there not grim humor and bitter rebuke in Jesus' condemnation of those who thought that God would hear them for their much speaking, or those who put a gloomy look on their face to impress others with their fasting?

Yes, just as there is humor and laughter and mirth every- where, so there is in Galilee. The sensitivity of Jesus could turn any situation, even the most trying, to the advantage of his teaching and his cause either by humor or by force- ful and penetrating words.

Much of Jesus' sense of the incongruous in life was turned to the abuse of wealth perpetrated by the rich. He saw an irony in the rich man's care for his possessions which are not only of no permanent value, but actually more often a hindrance to the realization of life's abiding values. How well this is illustrated in one of his memorable stories.

"A rich man had land which bore good crops. He began to think to himself, 'I don't have a place to keep all my crops. What can I do? This is what I can do,' he told himself; 'I will tear down my barns and build bigger ones, where I will store the grain and all my other goods. Then I will say to myself: Lucky man! You have all the good things you need for many years. Take life easy, eat, drink, and enjoy yourself!' But God said to him, 'You fool! This very night you will give up your life; then who will get all these things you have kept for yourself?'" (Luke 12:16-20)

And Jesus concluded, "This is how it is with those who pile up riches for themselves but are not rich in the sight of God."

SECTION XI

JESUS

XI. JESUS

1. Jesus, a Fact in History
2. Jesus, the Son of God
3. Jesus, the Son of Man
4. Jesus Made Religion Relevant
5. Jesus' Supreme Contribution to Life

1. JESUS, A FACT IN HISTORY

Jesus stands out as a fact in history. The appearance of Jesus, having a date in time and a place in history, is no isolated event but a fact in history which claims man's fullest attention. It is not an accident but an illumination of a Light, a Power, a Love always present and made real in a life like our own, having found a heart pure enough, a mind clear enough, a soul courageous enough to make itself known and its influence forever felt. No haphazard universe could produce such a personality. Only in a cosmic order which is motivated by law, back of which is a great Mind, could such a figure of heroic moral goodness appear.

Students of the life, the teachings and the spirit of Jesus have seen in the advent of Jesus not an unrelated event nor a solitary fact; rather, they have seen in his life the high peak of a long ascending process, the beginning of a new order of life, revealing broader dimensions and greater possibilities in the quality of personality and the refinement of the human spirit. They saw a lonely, lovely person walking the pathway of all humanity who, in the fullness of time, reveals the possibilities awaiting all those who live in the way of the Power in which men live and move and have their being. They recognized in him a new beginning, a new epoch, dividing the history of humanity into before and after.

What was the fact underlying the scholar's interpretation? It has been well stated by a leading scholar, a man of science and a follower of the Way.

While yet humanity was in its childhood, there appeared in Palestine one who in his personal life exhibited perfect manhood, whose life was full of the most complete internal harmony, liberty and independence. He realized that toward which the whole revolutionary process has evidently been tending. His appearance, which is the most remarkable fact in human history is of the same order as the appearance of personality in life; it marked a new era in history. In him civilization moved from the self-regarding basis to an other-regarding basis. Love came for the first time to perfect and victorious expression, with the result that his personality and teaching thereafter acted as a transforming, elemental energy in the world. In direct relation to him men of all races have found they are freed from tormenting inner dualism, and began to become masters of themselves through the moral and spiritual power of his life and spirit.

The above statement is a resume of J. Y. Simpson's *Man and the Attainment of Immortality*, Chapter II, acceptable to anyone who has a sense of the reality of history. It is a matter of simple fact that with the advent of Jesus there came a new level into the life of humanity, a new power released, a new law revealed: the law of love. If we are to know the real meaning and purpose of life, it will come through obedience to this law. Thus, man will leave behind his lowly beginnings and rise to his true destiny.

We are the children of God, born out of the heart of this amazing universe, in it and of it, earth of its earth, spirit of its spirit; in our infinitely ranging minds a tiny ray of light which searches out life's secrets; in our hearts a quest to know, to become, to realize life abundant; in our spirits a sure sense of beauty, of wonder, of immortality, of eternity. And at the center of our life is the radiant figure of Jesus, humanity's greatest personality and its loftiest spirit, in whom is "life, and the life is the light of men."

2. JESUS, THE SON OF GOD

Jesus has about him a divinity which my intellect cannot fathom, but which my heart can understand.

Somehow, it is impossible for me personally, and for our world, to dispense with Jesus because he gave to us the clearest portrayal of the power in which we live and move and have our being—God. Still more, he has given to us the clearest meaning of the purpose of human existence, a meaning and purpose for life—my life and, I would hope, your life as well as the life of all humanity.

No one needs to prove to me the existence of God. In fact, Emmanuel Kant long ago illustrated for us by the use of the most watertight logic that intellectually it is impossible to prove the existence or the non-existence of God. Faith need not rest upon intellectual arguments. My faith in God rests upon foundations so deep that I have no fear that this universe will vanish in a senseless dream. My sense of being a part, if only a small part, of this universe, my awareness of my life's very being as a part of a power not of myself, and my reverence for my own and all human destiny—all that is within that looks up and out and on—fills my consciousness with an inspiring awareness that I am a creature of a reality whose marvelous creativity and nature and ultimate purpose are beyond my finding out.

154 LIFE'S ABIDING RESOURCES

Then, you ask me, how are we to think of this reality? Here, I grant, we become involved in well-nigh insurmountable difficulties. How is man, so infinite and transient, whose contact with reality is but for "three score years and ten," to even think of the Alpha and the Omega who brought the worlds into being, and whose spirit motivates a universe where time is timeless and space is spaceless, and whose very existence is infinite, without beginning and without end?

As I see it, only as we can see in our humanity a life which lends itself to intellectual interpretation and emotional stability, to all that enhances life—the good, the beautiful and the true—can we begin to comprehend that reality. I hold that in Jesus, and in Jesus alone, we have such a life. Jesus gives to me and, I would hope, to you the clearest vision of God. He so lived the spirit of God in human life that he could say with all confidence, yet humility, "I and the Father are one." The ages past have seen in him the revelation of God. Our age must continue to do so; for he is the answer to humanity's longings and to the individual's heartcry for life at its best, and for a sense of oneness with life's ultimate reality. He lived a faith which can remove mountains; he held a hope for worthy human destiny; and he gave a love which can bind all humanity into a brotherhood of man through the Fatherhood of God. And God "has made from one every nation of men to live on all the face of the earth, . . . in the hope that they might feel after him and find him. Yet he is not far from each of us; for . . . 'In him we live and move and have our being'." (Acts 27:26-28)

In Jesus we can best see God.

> That one Face, far from vanishes, rather grows,
> Or decomposes but to recompose,
> Becomes my universe that feels and knows.
>
> *—Browning*

3. JESUS, THE SON OF MAN

In a quiet moment Jesus asked his disciples, "Who do men say that the Son of Man is?"

Our age still asks that question: "Who do men say the Son of Man is?" The Lenten days should challenge us to more careful and realistic thinking about Jesus and the tremendous influence of his life and teachings and spirit upon the whole life of man.

All thoughtful men would agree with Ernest Renan who weighed critically any concession to Christianity as in his *Vie de Jesus* he wrote, "Whatever may be the unexpected phenomena of the future, Jesus will not be surpassed. His worship will constantly renew itself. His history will provoke endless tears, his sufferings will subdue the stoutest hearts; all ages will proclaim that, among the sons of men, no one has been born who is greater than Jesus."

Multitudes have held and still want to hold to Jesus as the Son of God. Yet they are filled with conflicting emotions when wondering whether Jesus is human or divine.

When our age, characterized by science as a world held together with the life within it, created and motivated by cosmic laws, tries for a more realistic understanding of Jesus which will not be in conflict with the known processes of life, it confronts confusing difficulties. These difficulties arise over the error of not realizing the inherent unity of the human and the divine. For, in reality, ours is a universe; as such it has not two sources but one source of creation. There is a unity in all life. It was with rare insight that the Psalmist, referring to man, wrote, "Thou has made him a little less than God," as did also Paul when he wrote, "We know we shall be like him."

We, like the early followers of Jesus, find ourselves confronted with intellectual difficulties when we try to determine whether Jesus is human or divine. Two of the gospel writers felt it necessary to write of a virgin birth of Jesus. (Or was it later writers?) Two others did not make such an approach. And Jesus never referred to a miraculous birth to attest to his divinity. He always spoke and thought of his oneness with the spirit of God. Thinking in this manner with Jesus, we also rid ourselves of the difficulty of holding to a belief of Jesus as God or of his preexistence.

When the writer of the Fourth Gospel wrote, "In the beginning was the Word," his purpose was not primarily to state the pre-existence of Jesus, but rather to make Jesus and his teachings acceptable to the thought of life of the Greco-Roman people. He sought to do this by identifying Jesus with the Ephesian (Greek) philosophy of the "Logos" (Word), "The Essence of Life." And the first eighteen verses of the Gospel According to John are a prologue for this purpose, and the whole purpose of this Gospel was to make the more Jewish Gospels of Matthew and Mark more acceptable to the Gentiles.

In the final analysis, if we are to come to a more realistic and meaningful understanding of Jesus, through which we can make him and his teachings more relevant to our modern world, we must identify ourselves more deeply with the spirit of Jesus and its impact upon the life of his times. With us, as with the early disciples, the way to an acceptance of the humanity and the divinity of Jesus is to open our life to the impact of his spirit upon us. The testimony of the centuries is that to feel the full impact of his life involves the recognition that he is at once the Son of God and the Son of Man.

To return to Renan's *Life of Jesus*, when he describes Calvary, he addresses the Man on the Cross in these terms of passionate recognition: "Thou art destined to become the cornerstone of humanity in such wise that to tear Thy name from this world would be to shake it to its foundations."

4. JESUS MADE RELIGION RELEVANT

Jesus was repulsed by the barrenness and the super-
ficiality of the lives he found men of his day living. So
much of the religious life was formal, ritualistic, ceremonial, having little to do with morality. The Pharisees were a
pious lot. Theirs was a legalistic religion. Orthodoxy in
Jesus' day expressed itself in many external rites, such as,
ceremonial washings, restrictions about eating, ridiculously
trivial tithing, ceremonial Temple sacrifices. The teaching
of the Rabbis, both oral and written, included hundreds
of senseless prohibitions, greatly complicating the ancient
Hebrew law and making life a burden, all of which had
little to do with character and righteousness.

Jesus lived spiritually in a different world. He held that
righteousness is moral; not ritual, but character. His test
of goodness is the motive of the heart. As the heart, even
the life must be; for out of the overflow of the heart come
the issues of life. Goodness comes from the inner life of a
person. Get the ideals, the attitudes, the purposes right
and character will result.

The great lasting value of Jesus' wisdom on the meaning
and the importance of righeousness lies in the deep nature
of his thinking. He never dealt with surface details. He
did not clutter up his teachings with complicated codes of
conduct. Rather he illuminated a few fundamental points
at issue, and clarified a few basic principles and the eternal
values involved in them. He challenged men to be perfect
as their Creator is perfect. True, this leaves much spiritual
questing for men, but Jesus' was an ongoing, eternal Gospel
as applicable to our century as to his own.

If Jesus were moving about amid our life today, he
would repudiate much of what passes for his religion. He
would sweep aside any form or tradition or ceremony if
it did not contribute to the abundant life of man. We to-

day quibble much over theological definitions and ecclesiastical orders which have little to do with securing
the abundant life for all. Imagine Jesus, if you can, en-
gaging in such controversies. It is absolutely opposed to
his spirit.

How irreligious it is for men today to be quibbling over
form when humanity is lying bleeding at the roadside;
when leaders of nations are sparring with each other for
power while victims of man's inhumanity to man are
maimed and killed by the modern ingenuity of war; when
violence and evil are conspiring against the spiritual life of
man; when human souls are languishing in their thirst for
the way of the creative God. So often we view the absurd
spectacle of men engaged in long, bitter controversy over
some dogma of bygone days, yet refuse to raise their voices
on some great moral issue lest they lose their influence or
their job.

May the eyes of our soul be opened to see things of abiding worth! May we strive to know and to understand and
to follow the "only true God and Jesus Christ whom he
has sent, for this is life eternal!"

We would cry out with Channing Pollock: "If we would
only unwrap all the red-tape from about Jesus and hold
him up as he is, he would draw the whole world unto
him." The world, according to Channing Pollock's play,
"The Fool," calls man a fool who follows Jesus' way.
But after all who is the fool? Surely, not the man who
consecrates himself to the good of his fellow men. The
wise man seeks out and follows the truth which makes
men free. Jesus is the way and the truth and the life
which will lead humanity to life that is abundant and
eternal.

5. JESUS' SUPREME CONTRIBUTION TO LIFE

Jesus' supreme contribution to mankind is the new and magnificent meaning he gave to life. He invested human activity with a new and meaningful significance. He taught that every man was a potential son of the creative God, and that every man's life and activity relates to the abiding realm of God.

Men live and work and serve best when their life is seen and felt to have deep meaning and worthy purpose. It was with such meaningful and purposeful lives that Jesus set out to form a new society, "the kingdom of God." He taught that the way of truth would lead to an abundant life, that the way of truth would free men from the shackles of the past and give to their life a greater freedom and a new significance. This way would not be easy; it would often call for courageous self-sacrifice; but, in the end, it would lift humanity to new levels of achievement. He taught that he who seeks the old selfish ways of power and prestige loses his true self, his soul; but he who loses himself in the quest for real life will find his soul, find life that is abundant and eternal. This is basic in the way of Christianity. Christianity quests unwaveringly for spiritual goals which lead to worthy human destiny.

It is here that the way of Jesus has so much to contribute to life. When a man dreams his dreams and sets his goals before him and dedicates himself to their realization, Jesus, his teachings, his life and his spirit set the course for their fulfillment. His way of life leads to the unfolding of life's meaning and purpose and joy. One's life and work take on a meaningful significance.

Jesus came that men might have life, and that they might have it more abundantly. Those who will follow his way find that all great living is a creative art; all noble living is the result of the worthy meanings which motivate us, and the noble purposes which inspire our quest. To help men and women to achieve this abundant living, to help them find life's deeper meaning, and to help them to share this abundant life with its deeper meaning with others in terms of work and service and character, to the end that all may cooperatively achieve life that is real and eternal—for this Jesus lived and for this he gave his life. This is the new and significant content which he contributed to life. This is the life to which he calls us.

Courageously and with consecration to enter into adventurous living and serving by following ideal after ideal, value after value until those are found that lead us to the joy and peace and love that lift life ever higher, and give the human personality mastery over the things which are temporal—this is the dream of dreams come to fulfillment. This is the joy that Jesus has set before us. This is the gospel of Jesus. With this kind of living the kingdom of God is within the realm of the possible.

SECTION XII

LIFE

XII. LIFE

1. Life Is Exhilarating
2. Life's Fundamental Purpose
3. Don't Sell Yourself Short
4. Slow Me Down, Lord
5. When the Going Gets Rough
6. Restructuring Our Lifestyle

1. LIFE IS EXHILARATING

Life—this marvelous, this mysterious, this miraculous thing we call life—is exhilarating.

When I look out from my window, I see a great majestic oak tree towering skyward like a high green mountain whose top seems to touch the fleecy white clouds as they gently drift by. Then at night, when the stars come out, my thoughts go beyond the tree and the clouds, and I try to break through the infinity of the universe. Humility forces me to a proper perspective which calls forth introspection of that deep within which we call the soul. Here a soul, a being, a person is set in the midst of time and eternity. How can anyone feel other than overwhelmed with wonder and gratitude.

God through the mystery of his marvelous creativity has placed us in a universe that is so precisely ordered that it creates energy, beauty and love. We are a vital part of this universe. We are creatures of it. We are one with it. We are one with the creator, God.

It is exhilarating to realize that the same processes which motivate me activate the beautiful cardinal as he flits about in the tree. Similarly the same process gives growth to the tree. It is all so marvelous, so exhilarating, this process which we call life. A tiny seed starts to grow sending out its roots and branches, surging up through silt and soil,

> "An instinct within that reaches and towers,
> And, groping blindly above it for light,
> Climbs to a soul in grass and flowers."

The tree is composed of the same elements as the bird and I, principally of oxygen, nitrogen, hydrogen and carbon, until at length, through a marvelous process of growth, it becomes a thing of beauty and majesty, and akin to all life. It is not strange that St. Francis of Assisi, so attuned to his world, considered the birds and animals his brothers. We are all not only with all creatures but also with all creation inextricably enmeshed.

To contemplate deeply being a part of this mysterious universe, with its vast galaxies of stars and the planets as well as the earth made beautiful by its mountains and rivers and oceans, this is continuously exhilarating.

The great wonder of it all comes only to those who will seriously contemplate and grasp the fact that through the diversity of our universe there runs a unifying, *creative synthesis* that makes one akin to the atoms, the plants and the animals; and that the *creative synthesis* moves all creation up and on to more perfect life.

Yet the greatest exhilaration comes,

> When I consider thy heavens, the work of thy fingers
> The moon and the stars which thou hast formed;

and I contemplate the question,

> What is man that thou shouldst think of him,
> And the son of man that thou shouldst care for him?

> Yet thou has made him a little lower than God,
> And dost crown him with glory and honor!

What may yet lie ahead in the infinite range of the human mind and in the possibilities of the personality and in the soul of man is beyond our comprehension.

How exhilarating to realize that in my Father's universe there are many wonderful possibilities, "many mansions." The way of Jesus is the way to the fullest realization.

2. LIFE'S FUNDAMENTAL PURPOSE

Why Life? What do men live for? What is the purpose of your life and of mine? What is the meaning of human existence? Is our purpose in life aligned with all life's fundamental purpose? What is life all about? What is its end, its purpose?

These are searching questions. The deepest question which comes to any man or woman who thinks is this question of the purpose of life, especially his life or her own life. There must be a purpose, a meaning why men live. If not, life has no meaning.

This world and its life is ever evolving, coming up out of the vast void, surging on into struggling elements, uniting into chemical and biological units, creating ever higher levels of being, until it crowns itself in man. Man is more than matter and physical; he is dreams, ideals, personalities, and, most important, the spirit of man. Thus life evolves from matter up through the animal, through levels of intelligence and personality toward the spiritual. If, as the trend of creative evolution indicates, life has been moving up from the material to the spiritual, may we not then state the purpose of the creative God as the desire to bring the spiritual to triumphant supremacy over the material.

This is the theme of Jesus' teaching. Jesus taught, "Seek first the realm (kingdom) of God and his righteousness." "God," to Jesus, "is spirit." Man's supreme quest must, then, be the realization of God's spirit in life, the realization of the spiritual life. This was Jesus' supreme passion: "I came that men may have life, and have it abundantly." "To this end was I born, and for this cause came I into the world, that I should bear witness to truth." And the ultimate truth back of our universe rests in God.

The supreme purpose of Jesus, the very end of his existence is the attainment of the spiritual life, the understanding of God, and the realization of the spirit of God in the life of man. The ultimate goal of all human life is the achieving of life that is real, abundant and eternal, life that even death cannot destroy, and that can outlast all time and eternity.

In order to bring about the triumph of the spiritual over the material, God has created in this universe the spirit of man, and has given to men freedom to carry on the struggle unaided by any intervention, save through the realm of the spiritual. The struggle of spirit over matter, then, is carried on through the cooperation of the spirit of man with the spirit of God.

What a magnificent and inspiring challenge there is in this conception! God depends upon man for the fulfillment of His purpose. Apart from man in his heroic struggle, the great purpose of God is unfulfilled. The triumph of the spiritual will come when man has learned to put himself in harmony with the purpose of God as His creative spirit and power moves on through the cosmic process.

3. DON'T SELL YOURSELF SHORT

Although a person's life is not measured in dollars and cents, one should not sell one's self short. Unfortunately, in our materialistic age we all too often bow to the people of great wealth. But the extent of a person's accomplishments is seldom, if ever, measured by the amount of money he possesses. Multitudes of the selfish rich have passed on and are forgotten for they have left nothing of abiding value. This is not to say, however, that all wealthy people make no contribution to life; there have been those who have made our world a much better place in which to live because of the great contribution they have made.

Nevertheless, do not sell yourself short. As the old saying goes, don't hide your talent under a bushel. Many of our talents escape our notice completely. Only in later years, or only when others disclose them, are these achievements known. Our records abound with innumerable examples.

Recall the life of Mozart, the great Austrian composer. Mozart died at the age of thirty-five—in abject poverty. His wife did not have enough money to buy a coffin for his body, and the cheap wooden box which she finally secured was a gift of charity. On the way to the grave, the driver of the hearse learned that he would not receive the customary gratuity, and instantly began to curse the dead man. To this day no one knows where the body of Mozart was finally laid.

At the time of Mozart's death, his achievements must have seemed insignificant, and Mozart, dying in obscurity, may have seemed, to the few about him, a pathetic failure. His real accomplishments at the time remained small and unnoticed. But not so today—his great compositions are receiving well-deserved praise and recognition, and will continue to reveal themselves as the years roll into centuries. The real Mozart will be remembered for his great compositions of music although his final resting place is unknown.

So you, dear reader, may feel that you have accomp-

lished little of abiding value during hard and difficult
days of striving. But do not sell yourself short. Your real
accomplishments may have passed by unnoticed by you
and your contemporaries. Later years may bring out their
true worth. Not many flowers are "born to blush unseen
and waste their sweetness on the desert air." Many a
beautiful personality has lived the whole life through
without ever knowing the lasting influence for good on the
life of others. This is so true of parents and teachers.
Many parents live and toil for their children and pass out
and on, and only after it is too late do their children come
to realize how much the precious value of their parents'
spirit gave to their lives.

I recall two teachers whose beautiful and understanding
spirit meant so much to me in the formative years of my
early schooling. I can never forget their beautiful personality. I did not think so much about it then, but the
memory of their kind understanding remains with me always. My regret is that they passed on without knowing
how much their efforts in my behalf meant to me. I can
never forget the school principal who, because of his faith
in boys, made a decision one day as I sat in
his office which did much to shape the course of my life.
I did have the opportunity, years later, as he sat in my congregation one Sunday, to let him know what his faith and
his spirit meant not only to me but, also, to other boys
who passed through his schools.

Also, I am thinking of a retired school teacher who has
always sold herself short. She is kind, gentle, generous and
likeable. Because of her unusually deep interest in her
pupils, she has made a large and lasting contribution to
many a life. Among her other fine accomplishments,
she has also fine artistic talents. Yet, all her life she has
been living with a sense of inferiority.

Yes, so many of us, even many ministers, perhaps even
you, have been selling yourself short.

Invisible as the wind, blowing stray seeds,
Life breathes on life, though ignorant of what it brings,
And spirit touches spirit on the strings
Where music is. O we have failed and failed,
And never known if we or the world failed,
Clouded and thwarted—yet, perhaps,
The best of all we do and dream of lives—unguessed.
                                        —*Laurence Binyon*

4. SLOW ME DOWN, LORD

This story was told of Huxley, the philosopher. He was scheduled to give a lecture in Dublin. Hurriedly, on the appointed morning, he took a train. Arriving late at Dublin, Huxley rushed off the train, through the station, and, seeing a waiting cab, jumped in and shouted to the driver, "Drive Fast." After rattling over the rocky streets of Dublin for some time and gaining his breath, Huxley said to the cab driver, "Say, do you know where you are going?" To which the cabby replied, "I don't know where I am going, but I am driving fast."

This is a picture of our civilization. We are driving fast, but do we know where we are going? Our life—the life all about us—moves at a rapid pace. We need to slow down. It takes a heart attack to slow some of us down. Others are rushing toward one. We would be wise to slow down. We could get places faster and farther if we had the sense to slow down. But thousands rush along our expressways at 70 and 80 miles an hour. When many see a sign, "Slow Down," they are ready to "blow their top." They cannot understand why some dangerous sections are marked "Speed Limit, 50 MPH." Slow us down, Lord, slow us down!

Thousands of men and women are getting up early every morning and rushing to work (when the traffic jams do not slow them down). They work hard all day to make money and sit up half the night spending it, without taking time to ask the question of what it is all about. Slow us down, Lord, slow us down!

We must take time to stop, look and listen, a time to pause and look into the meaning of life and to find its purpose, a time to think more deeply on the finer and the fundamental values of life.

All of us really need some fisherman's rock, some lakeside or sandy beach where alone we can have time to think on the abiding values of life—our life—where we can share with God "the silence of eternity, interpreted by love." Jesus suggested that, "when you pray, go into your room, and shut the door and pray to your Father who is in secret; and your Father who sees in secret will reward you."

It is recorded of Jesus that he sought out the quiet hills and the silence of the night, where alone, he felt the touch of the eternal spirit of God. In times of crisis he spent the whole night in prayer. Out of these periods he came refreshed. Out under the stars and in the silence of the night made Jesus what he was to men and women. Out of these periods of silence and solitude the world's greatest religion was born. Only those who wait and pray, who watch and work, are God's great secrets of the resources of power revealed. Slow us down, Lord, slow us down!

> "Slow me down, Lord!
> Ease the pounding of my heart
> By the quieting of my mind.
> Steady my hurried pace
> With a vision of an eternal reach of time

Give me,
Amidst the confusion of my day,
The calmness of the everlasting hills.
Break the tension of my nerves
With the soothing music of the singing streams
That live in my memory,
Help me to know
The magic restoring power of sleep.
Teach me the art
Of making minute vacations of slowing down
    to look at a flower,
    to chat with an old friend or
    make a new one.
    To pat a stray dog,
    to watch a spider build a web,
    to smile at a child,
    to read a few lines
    from a book.

Remind me each day
That the race is not always with the swift;
That there is more to life than
    increasing its speed.

Let me look upward
Into the branches of the towering oak
And know that it grew great and strong
Because it grew slowly and well.

Slow me down, Lord,
And inspire me to send my roots deep
Into the soil of life's enduring values,
That I may grow toward the stars
Of my greater destiny.

                      —*O. L. Crain*

5. WHEN THE GOING GETS ROUGH

There is the story of a dog whose favorite sport was chasing cats. But once in a great while, by some super-canine burst of speed, he would overtake the cat. The dog would sit down and begin to scratch fleas, for, when he came upon the cat, he had neither the technique nor the appetite to complete the undertaking.

When the going gets rough, what is one to do? When life and its duties face hard days, what is one to do? Turn back or run away from the difficulties? Only the cowardly do that.

Sit in a rocking chair and close one's eyes and hope for some turn of events to remove the difficulty? Only the wishful thinker does that. Cry out in despair, wring one's hands? Only the childish do that. Sit down and scratch fleas? Only dogs do that.

Such questions demand positive answers, for upon their answers depends our attitude toward life. This is a time when one's religion is helpful. The Bible is replete with the experiences of people who knew life when the going was rough. Yet with faith and courage they pressed forward into the way ahead. The first steps may have been hard, but they brought forth a surge of newfound strength. Life became easier.

Abraham went out not knowing whither he went. Joseph, though thrown into prison, kept his life high with integrity and courage. Moses, though confronted with discouraging difficulties, kept his people moving toward the promised land. Amos, confronted with the injustices against the people, moved fearlessly against intrenched injustices of his day. Jesus set his face steadily toward Jerusalem. When one stands up to one's clear duty, although confronted by great difficulties, fears fade away, and there comes an inner strength and courage with its sustaining power.

This is the way of life. Mankind has been created and conditioned to go the hard way. The creative God has marvelously fashioned man. The hard way creates strength. Difficulties move men and women from strength to strength. Tried souls who face life in the hard days find a reservoir of strength and courage only awaiting to be released.

Jesus said, "The way to life is hard." The easy way often leads to defeat and, in the end, to destruction. The difficult, the hard, the seemingly impossible way challenges the best within one. "You will have trouble," said Jesus, "but take courage, I have overcome the world." He implies that we, too, can triumph.

Helen Keller, who was no stranger to a life filled with great difficulties, once wrote; "The struggle which evil necessitates is one of the greatest blessings. It makes us all strong, patient, helpful men and women. It lets us into the soul of things and teaches us that, although the world is full of suffering, it is also full of overcoming it."

When the going gets rough, don't stop; move straight ahead with trust in your Creator who will not let you down. Then you are ready for high adventure. God moves on with you.

6. RESTRUCTURING OUR LIFESTYLE

Those who take a deeper and more careful look at life as a whole in our generation must realize that the problems which perplex us are fraught with far-reaching destiny. The crisis about which we hear so much these days is of a greater magnitude and a far more fundamental character than the crisis in oil and energy. The problems of our time lie deep in the complex trend of life everywhere. Our generation is confronted with an unprecedented rate of change in the economic, social, political and technological spheres. Much of this change has already caused far-reaching disturbances not only in our Western Hemisphere, but also in Europe, Asia and Africa.

The crucial, continuing crisis confronting us goes to the very heart of life. Science and technology have placed in the hands of this generation almost unlimited power, both for creativity and for destruction. The development of the atomic bomb placed civilization at the crossroads. Two ways lie before us: construction or destruction. This generation is confronted with choice between creativity or continuing crisis. In the words of a great and wise ancient leader: "Behold, I have set before you this day life and death, therefore, choose life." Have we the wit and the wisdom and the intelligence to choose life?

Let us look carefully at the character of the trend of life socially, economically and idealogically. The trend of our life is basically selfish, self-seeking. Individually we want the highest wages, the best paying job, the largest return on our investments. Many professionals place salary above service. Corporations are spurred on by the profit motive. As the head of one of the large oil corporations, at the beginning of the oil crisis, admitted, "Our gasoline tanks are empty not because of the lack of oil supply, but because of the lack of profits." In our highly competitive society, corporations cannot exist without profits. Nations cooperate with each other on the basis of "enlightened self-interest." This is our lifestyle today.

It is ironic that, in an age when the intelligence of mankind has reached the highest point yet recorded, nations all around the earth are approaching a crisis of disastrous proportions. Surely, the amazing amount of information possessed by man and the immense means and the technological skills that can be mobilized would justify the hope that all this power would be used for the fundamental betterment of all humanity.

However, all the intellectual genius of man and all the resources of life-perpetuating energy are of small avail unless they are motivated by sound moral, ethical and spiritual principles. Yet the fact remains that our world societies are motivated by self-interest. Moreover, our great industrial enterprises operate wastefully and encourage unnecessary consumption. The people consume the earth's resources luxuriously and often prodigally in selfish living, indifferent to the waste and the depletion of the resources of this good earth. All through the age of abundance, men have lacked the wisdom to co-exist peacefully on this small and vulnerable planet. Shall we continue along our thoughtless way? Will our selfish lifestyle be continued?

Surely modern man must possess the intelligence to see that our world society is thwarted and often torn asunder by the continually increasing and intolerable disparity in the living standards and opportunities among the world's people. The self-interest of nations creates conflicts. Hundreds of men, women and children live in poverty without occupation or possibility of development. Natural resources are pillaged, the air we breathe and the water we drink are increasingly polluted for the benefit of the few and to the detriment of the many with little thought given to the generations to come.

The magnitude of the continuing crisis will be greatly aggravated if there is any truth to the prediction that the world population will double in another century. If the present selfish trend in modern society persists, and if no efforts are made to restructure them toward new ideals and goals, they could bring disaster to mankind's future.

Nothing short of the restructuring of the trends of human living will set humanity on toward its worthy future. Selfishness and self-interest on the part of individuals and nations must be replaced by altruism and interest in the welfare of all. The service motive must be given priority over profits. Cooperation must replace competition. Love must triumph over hate and motivate the hearts of men and women and shape the life of nations.

The late Dr. Frank Laubach has said, "If we are to change the direction of the world, many more of us must take the whole world into our hearts and begin to work for the welfare of mankind." The Church and leaders of religion everywhere must lead the way. Vast changes with far-reaching destiny lie ahead. Wholesome direction is needed. At this moment in history multitudes are confused and frustrated and longing for a change for something better.

If the selfish, the unwholesome and the frustrating aspects of our life are to be replaced by the good, the true and the lovely, if our individual lives are to have poise, purposefulness and peace, we must earnestly, seriously give precedence to the eternal over the temporal, the spiritual over the material. The spiritual values must be placed above all other concerns. We must pursue purposely the lovely, the true, the beautiful. We must league ourselves with the eternal rather than build our homes, our lives and our temples on the shifting sands; for "man shall not live by bread alone, but by every word that proceeds forth from the mouth of God."

SECTION XIII

LOVE

XIII. LOVE

1. The Power of Love
2. Love, the Conquering Power
3. Can Love Be Treason?
4. Love Is Stronger Than Death
5. That Without Which

1. THE POWER OF LOVE

As one reads the gospel story with discernment, it will be recognized as the story of the struggle to the death of the forces of evil with the power of love, the conflict between the love of power and the power of love, the contest between the material and the spiritual. To use Jesus' words, it is the choice between "God and Mammon."

The Jewish people, in Jesus' time, looked for a Messiah who would deliver them. They pictured him as a perfectly good Servant and a perfectly powerful King. Jesus realized that such a combination was impossible. This was the issue he struggled with in the Wilderness. Should he seek to lead the people by turning the stones into bread to feed them, or by dazzling miraculous powers, or by joining the Zealots and leading a rebellion against Rome? When he came out of the Wilderness "in the power of the spirit," it was with the conviction that he would seek to lead by the way of love.

This conflict is seen in its most intense form in Gethsemane. The choice was not between two alternative courses of action, either of which could win a following. The issue was: power that could destroy or love that would die. Had love reached a limit beyond which it could not go? Could love accept even the worst? When man's evil is at its worst, how great is love?

The issue was settled for once and for all time when

Jesus arose from his knees in Gethsemane and went with courage to his trial and the Cross. God's love is infinite. Nothing that men could do to God would destroy God's forgiving love.

This is the heart of the gospel of Christianity. Jesus sent his disciples out to preach this gospel with the "remission of sin." God so loved mankind that not even the Cross could destroy His love. If love triumphed then, it triumphs now. The Cross, the symbol of God's love, is the "power of God." It's gospel is "the power of God for salvation to everyone who has faith." If one is to be defeated and destroyed, it is against a love like that.

But even a love like that cannot save one who rejects it. If we insist on aligning ourselves with evil, if we insist on ignoring God's love, if we continue to be indifferent to God's way of love, then we are defeated; for God's way of love is the way to triumphal living.

So, we would do well to contemplate the meaning of the Cross of Christ. The conflict out of which it issues is still in our world. It is the conflict between good and evil, between God and materialism, between Christ and Caesar. "Thanks be to God who gives us the victory through our Lord Jesus Christ."

Love's way is the way to life—life that is real, abundant, eternal.

2. LOVE, THE CONQUERING POWER

"A New commandment I give to you, that you love one another; as I have loved you, that you also love one another," said Jesus.

There is no other note in the religion of Jesus that can strike deeper into the alleviation of the ills of men and bring men closer to security, peace and the abundant life than can this note of love which Jesus sounded in this new commandment.

We may try other emphases, other ways of life; we may forget or ignore the new commandment; but, at long last, love will emerge from the severest test as the triumphant conqueror. Given a family, a church, a school, a factory, a community or a nation where people live in love, there will be found life, and life abundant.

This was illustrated to me in a never-to-be-forgotten way during my service in the Near East following World War I. Into the home of one of our American educators, there came from one of the orphanages a young Armenian girl. She helped in this home and attended a mission school. One day there was entertained at dinner in this home, a Turkish friend of ours, R———— Bay. As this Armenian girl came into the dining room to serve the food, she uttered a cry of alarm, and, dropping the tray she was carrying to the floor, fled from the room into the kitchen. When our hostess went into the kitchen, as I later learned, she discovered the girl in tears. The girl had recognized the Turkish guest as the officer in charge of the soldiers who had conducted the deportation in which her parents had lost their lives, and she had been deported from Armenia. Her first impulse this day was to seize a knife and rush back into the dining room to kill the Turk. But she recalled what she had learned in the mission school: "Love your enemy! If your enemy hunger feed him."

Love had conquered to save a life, and to redeem a soul!

3. CAN LOVE BE TREASON?

Resistance can be clarifying and cleansing in the life of a nation when its citizens have the courage to express the deep agonies of life. For instance, a recent play, in which the villain is a Stalinist Army lieutenant and the hero an ordinary young Russian soldier, has created quite a stir in Moscow's theatrical circles.

The play, written by Valentin Yezhov, winner of the Lenin Prize for drama, "The Night of the Nightingales," takes place at the end of World War II in a German town occupied by the Soviet troops. A young Russian soldier falls in love with a German girl and goes AWOL. They are caught together by the lieutenant, who is about to shoot the girl when the boy grabs his arm to prevent him from firing. The officer, angered by the young man's action, accuses him of treason against the state. The play then cautiously but firmly underscores the theme—*Can Love Be Treason!*

U.S. observers in Moscow, from whom I have drawn this report, state that audiences gasp at these scenes, realizing their deep implications for past and present in view of the millions executed and exiled under Stalin on the slightest pretext for "crimes against the state." The action of the play continues as a colonel debates the charges with the lieutenant as to whether the punishment proposed is not too severe.

"Why are you destroying this boy?" the colonel asks, as the audience applauds. The case is then taken to the commanding general who decides he must support the execution order. Finally the colonel, who is a tough fighting officer of the war, takes steps on his own not only to save the soldier's life but to send him home with his other comrades since the war is over. An aide then warns the colonel that he is jeopardizing his own career by going against the general's orders. The colonel replies that some place one must take a stand. "You let it drop once and then another time, and then nothing is left that is sacred. And one cannot live without something sacred. One simply cannot."

In the final scene the German girl makes an unusual concluding speech for the Russian stage—a prayer to God in which she cries, "God, you have seen everything. God, God! Do something so that people will no longer kill each other on earth."

How often in utter anguish the soul cries out to God for help! But why cry out thus to God? God needs us too. We would do well to remind ourselves of the note which Dag Hammarskjold wrote to himself on the eve of an important meeting of the Security Council of the United Nations: "Your responsibility is indeed terrifying. If you fail, it is God, thanks to your having betrayed Him, who will fail mankind. You fancy you can be responsible *to* God; can you carry the responsibility *for* God?"

"O Lord, help us to be masters of ourselves, that we may be servants of others." "Lord, make me an instrument of Thy peace."

4. LOVE IS STRONGER THAN DEATH

One of the most striking of modern stories is "The Bridge of San Luis Rey," by Thornton Wilder; so unique in its plot, so exquisite in its art, and so intriguing in its meaning.

The bridge of San Luis Rey collapsed and five people were hurdled to their death five hundred feet below. Why were these particular people thus to die? It is similar to the question we ask when someone near and dear to us is smitten by some dire mishap, filling us with mingled pity and dismay, often despair.

As the author tells the story of each of those five persons leading up to and ending in the tragedy, we seem to be left with the feeling that some divine motive may have been involved. Yet we rebel against such a suggestion. Thornton Wilder leaves so much for us to try to explain. So, the questioning haunts us still: Why those five and no others? Each one was found to be a person who had lavished his or her love upon someone, only to have loved in vain. This in itself is tragedy.

What is the meaning of it all?

It is all summed up in one illuminating last paragraph, and is formed in the mind of the saintly Madra Maria as she speaks words of hope and comfort to the sick in her hospital in Lima. "Even now," she thought, "almost no one remembers Esteban and Pepita but myself. Camila alone remembers her uncle Pio and her son; and this woman her mother. But soon we shall die and all memory of those five will have left the earth, and we ourselves shall be loved for a while and forgotten. But the love will have been enough; all those impulses of love will return to the love that made them. Even memory is not necessary for love. There is a land of the living and a land of the dead and the bridge is love, the only survival, the only meaning."

What haunting lines! If we could only fully comprehend them! They are trying to tell us what our hearts know to be true: "Love is stronger than death." All that God will keep and value, when He screens out the values of our days and years, is the love of our life with which we have blessed and hallowed our fellow men.

"The bridge is love, the only survival, the only meaning."

5. THAT WITHOUT WHICH

Men and nations have long sought a better way to human relations. The ancient Hebrews counselled wisdom: "Wisdom is the principle thing, therefore, get wisdom; and with all thy getting, get understanding." The Greeks sought knowledge and truth. The Romans placed their hopes on law. But satisfying human relationships with peace and security were never fully realized. One ancient prophet counselled justice, mercy and humility—all worthy virtues, but in themselves not sufficient to resolve the dilemmas of human relations.

Now in this dynamic twentieth century, we hear of much confidence expressed in science and technology and their ability to bring in a new day for mankind. At length, through science, the "new Messiah," it has been felt that the golden age would be ushered in. True, science and technology have been bringing in a whole new way of living by their transformation of our industrial order, and by relieving men of drudgery and burden of toil. They have greatly enhanced our modern life with the comforts, the conveniences and the gadgets of modern living.

But it must also be recognized that, as science was bringing in all this great advance in our industrial order, and technology transforming our way of living, they were also bringing in a whole new set of problems in the relationships of people who were trying to adjust themselves to the rapidly changing way of living. At the same time, science was slow in coming up with solutions to those personal and social and economic and even moral problems.

Scientific and technological advance has been nothing short of marvelous! Now at this moment in human history, characterized by differing ideologies, confusion and fears, when nations are seeking security against other nations, we see, once again, the concentration on science as the instrument of salvation. Clear thinking is needed desperately.

The emphasis on science and technology exalts force. It tends to confirm the popular conviction that force is the ultimate security. Our weaponry, so it is thought, must be so great that enemies are afraid to move against us. This fear creates hostility. Yet, we also are being warned that, to resort to force now, the instruments of warfare have become so destructive that they could bring irreparable disaster to mankind, if not annihilation.

We cannot rest our security upon weapons alone. We cannot acquiesce to the acceptance of hostility as the normal relationship of nations. We cannot surrender the hope that man can deal with his fellow men in faith and trust.

Christians may differ on the place of military strength in securing freedom, security and peace; but all agree that fear, hatred and hostility must not be the condition of mankind on this planet.

There is a better way. We must come to realize that, in addition to all the wonders which science has brought to our life, there is that without which man cannot have security, peace and life. This is what Christianity is trying to say to our world. "A new commandment give I unto you that you love one another." So taught Jesus.

Love is life's most essential quality, that without which all is futile. It is that quality in human life which marks one as a herald of a new and abiding social order. "If I speak with the tongues of men and angels, but have not love, I am a noisy gong or a clanging cymbal. And if I have prophetic powers, and understand all mysteries and all knowledge, and if I have all faith, so as to remove mountains, but have not love, I am nothing. If I give away all I have, and if I give my body to be burned, but have not love, I gain nothing."

We may have all the latest in modern weaponry, we may even have all the enlightened good will, we may send our food to the hungry of Asia and Africa, we may strengthen our Atlantic pacts, we may send our young men all around the world; but, if it lacks that without which all else fails— love—it profits us nothing. Love prompts respect for others. It holds to the rights of all peoples. It requires that whatsoever we would that others do to us, we do so to them. Love is humanity's highest hope.

"There are three things which last forever: faith, hope and love; but the greatest of them all is love."

SECTION XIV

MANKIND

XIV. MANKIND

1. The Measure of a Man
2. The Materialist
3. The Idealist
4. The Spiritual Man
5. The Christian
6. The Survival of Man

1. THE MEASURE OF A MAN

An old proverb in seeking to evaluate the character of a man suggests that "as a man thinketh in his heart, so he is." (Proverbs 23:7) Without getting involved in a discussion of whether action precedes thoughts or thoughts precede action, let us look more closely into this old proverb as a yardstick for the the measure of a man.

Modern Biblical scholars have variously translated this proverb. Here let it stand very much as it is, and seek to clarify its meaning. The phrase, "As a man thinketh," might well be stated: the estimate or the judgment of value, or the price put upon a thing. And the phrase, "in his heart," must also be clarified. The ancients used the word "heart" in a much more all inclusive sense than we do to-day. Heart was the seat of the emotions; but more, it was the seat of knowledge. It was almost equivalent of soul. "With the heart man believeth unto righteousness." "From the heart proceed the issues of life." Thus, in the heart, there is the mingling of emotion and knowledge, from which mingling comes a clearer insight into truth. Let this proverb, then, be considered thus: "As a man puts a price upon the things of his life, so he is." As he places a value or makes a judgment of worth on a thing, so is the measure of the man.

Here is a yardstick for the measure of a man. For as a man places a price on the things which he considered in his inmost life as vital, he thereby gives a means for the finding of his estimate of the relative value of the things of life, and his evaluation of the things of life gives us an estimate of the man himself.

Primitive man is first of all, and predominantly, an animal, ruled by his instincts, appetites and passions. His concern was chiefly a struggle for existence. The things of greatest value to him were food, comforts and pro-creation. It was only as he learned that there were other values that he rose higher to develop character and personality.

Civilized man, who is interested primarily in material things, is a *materialist*. Those who see beyond the material to the things of beauty, who see things not only as they are but as they ought to be, are *idealists*. The idealist values beauty and the arts and aspirations as of greater value. There are other persons whose ideals rise still higher. They have eyes to see the unseen. Justice, equity, freedom for all, love—these are the things of highest value. The man whose estimate of values go beyond the temporal to the eternal is a *spiritual* man. In our Christian civilization the outstanding personalities are those who commit themselves to the will and way of God as revealed in the teaching, the life and the spirit of Christ. This is the *Christian* man.

Every man reveals, through his interests and his values and his meanings, the dimension of his soul. How well this is illustrated by a story I picked up while living in the Indiana limestone country.

A man, while visiting a limestone quarry one day, paused to ask a workman what he was doing. The workman replied, "I'm cutting stone." A little further on he asked another workman, "What are you doing?" ("I'm working for $7.50 a day," was the reply.) When the man put the same question to a third stonecutter, this man answered, "I am helping to build a cathedral."

The estimate of value of the things of life, the meaning of life, is the measure of a man. The first stonecutter symbolizes a multitude who look at life uncomprehendingly. They are those for whom life is drudgery and meaningless. The second man symbolizes those who work for themselves. They work for pay, for power, for self. Their motives are material, transient, temporal. The third man symbolizes those who work for God and man, controlled by the ideals of beauty, goodness and truth. To them, life is a great and joyous adventure, and all work is creative cooperation in working out an infinite design of God for man.

2. THE MATERIALIST

Let us take the old proverb, "As a man thinketh in his heart, so he is," as a yardstick for the measure of a man. However, let it be stated a little more clearly as, "The price which a man is willing to pay for the things of his life, is the measure of the man."

The man who places the highest value on material things is a materialist. In his judgment the tangible is of greater value than the intangible. He is ruled by his instincts, his appetites and his passions. The materialist may be an intelligent person and not even acquire too great an advantage over others. He may be very likeable; a "hail fellow well met." He is predominantly a realist. He distrusts his ideals. He feels that they have little value in the hard world of things.

He places the highest value upon tangible wealth, possessions and the power that these provide. His quest for wealth and possessions and power fill his days. But these pass away all too soon.

Except a man have some sense of the meaning and worth of what he is doing, he will simply waste his life on material ends. He fails to build into his life the enduring values. If he wants to see life grow and thrill with a sense of real riches and power, he will not acquiesce to materialism, but will pay the self-giving price of a pioneer in heroically opening up a new approach to the real and abiding resources of this bountiful earth which has given him life and being.

When material things consume a man's time and energy, they shape his character and his life. When a man puts his highest estimate of value on material wealth and possessions, it is the real estimate of the man himself. For the price which a man is willing to pay for the things of his life is the measure of the man.

To illustrate, consider an amiable, even loveable materialist. One day Jesus was approached abruptly by a rich young man who had great possessions. The young man came to Jesus with the question: "Teacher, what good deed must I do, to have eternal life?" And Jesus said to him, "If you would enter life, keep the commandments." Then Jesus proceeded to remind him of the commandments having to do with life. But the young man said to him, "All these I have observed; what do I still lack?" And Jesus said to him, "If you would be perfect, go, sell what you possess and give to the poor, and you will have treasures in heaven; and come, follow me." When the young man heard this, he went away sorrowful; for he had great possessions.

This young man had a loveable, amiable personality. He evidently was a keen businessman with ability. He was capable of making an estimate of moral and material values. He knew a good thing when he saw it. His judgment must have been good, else he could not have had great possessions. He had good morals and worthy motives; he kept the commandments. But there was one thing which he lacked; commitment to the highest. He loved his possessions too much and valued them too highly. Before the Master he was called upon to make the greatest and the most far-reaching judgment of worth he had ever been called upon to make. On the one hand were his possessions, his wealth, his comforts; and, on the other hand, were the great eternal values which would create that life which is real, abundant and eternal. He chose the former, his possessions. In his estimate these material things were of greater value than the eternal. The giving up of eternal life was the price he was willing to pay to keep his possessions. He chose the things of a passing moment; and he like these passed into oblivion.

The price a man puts on the things of his life is the measure of the man.

3. THE IDEALIST

Every personal life is an adventure in creative living. Its ultimate aim is to produce something of great beauty, worth and enduring value. In order to follow through in this, man has become preeminently an idealizing creature. In following out his destiny, man has acquired the power to see things not only as they are but also as they ought to be. This ability to idealize gives meaning to much of the common things of life. Mere material things take on meaning, purpose and value.

When a man sees things in a setting of beauty and purpose and worth, we call him an idealist. He has risen above the material to see the eternal and abiding values. "The things that are seen are temporal, but the things which are not seen are eternal."

Life would have still remained dull and drab if man had not risen above hard realism and developed the ability to dream dreams and to see visions of the beauty and the splendor of his universe. This ability to see life through our ideals is what distinguishes man from the lower animals, for it fills him with the desire to make his dreams come true, thus creating in him the power of choice. His choices shape his life and character, and determine his destiny; for the price which a man is willing to pay for his ideals is the measure of the man.

The idealist rises above mere things. He sees the material things of his world not as ends but as means to worthy ends. The noble, the good, the beautiful and the true are basic in his very being. He has possibilities for good or evil. The possibilities are determined by what he does with his ideals.

A man like Woodrow Wilson came out of the World War I with his faith shattered in statesmanship as a way to bring international peace. He was convinced, and gave himself over in an effort to convince others that, "The sum of the whole matter is this, that our civilization cannot survive materially unless it be redeemed spiritually. It can be saved only by becoming permeated by the spirit of Christ and being made free in the practice which springs out of that spirit."

Wilson was truly an idealist. He had high ideals which he wished to see realized. He put forth every effort possible for their realization. In Paris he contended to have these ideals wrought into the final agreement. And it is only those who know something about the play of European diplomacy who are able to appreciate the degree to which he succeeded. He was not satisfied; not all had been gained. But what had been gained was worth struggling to retain.

At home in America his countrymen were not convinced

with the quality and quantity of the ideals gained in Paris. So, again under the strain of his office, Wilson set out on a tour of America to defend his ideals. Few men under as great a burden ever attempted a more trying task. He threw himself, body and soul, into a defense of his ideals. Every ounce of his energy, every resource of his intellect was given to his cause. Then, suddenly, one day, he collapsed. His nerves gave way. His powers snapped under the strain. They took him away with his body paralyzed, and his mind greatly impaired. It was the price which he was willing to pay. His energy, his intellect, his life—these were the price which he was willing to pay for his ideals.

The price which a man is willing to pay for his ideals is the true estimate of the value of the man.

4. THE SPIRITUAL MAN

A good man who can find him? His price is far greater than the most precious jewels. The heart of nations will trust him. He is the idealizing man who not only feels the worth of his ideals and the authority of his visions, but also he dedicates himself to their realization. Otherwise, he would simply remain an intelligent being not taking his idealizing powers seriously, but enjoying them and feeling that they were too good to be true. He is more than an idealist; he is a spiritual man.

The spiritual man seeks to harmonize his life with the "power in which men live and move and have their being." He seeks a oneness with the Essence of Life, the ultimate Reality, the creative God.

He lives the life of the spirit. The spiritual life rises above the lower order, above the animal, the brutal and the material. It seeks out the timeless, the enduring values. It finds its identity in character, personality, integrity, meekness, peace and love. Its deep concern is in the highest moral, ethical and spiritual values.

The spiritual man is characterized as one who places the highest estimate upon the timeless, the enduring, the eternal values. He shares the conviction that man does not live by bread alone, but by all that comes forth from the spirit of God.

He will be concerned with the highest moral and ethical life. He will champion progress and seek to advance movements for the welfare of his fellows. He will be even more, he will dream dreams and see visions of reforms, and he will work to project humanity far into the future. It takes prodigious amounts of work to put one's moral and ethical ideals into the form of character, and it takes super-human toil to transmute one's dreams of what life can be into reality. It takes courage and purpose, dynamic with idealism, to lift life to higher levels; but this heroic striving brings the thrill of creativity with the great Creator.

There are many illustrations of a spiritual man. Here we shall use one. Though he has passed from the world's scene over two decades ago, his name is still well known on every continent. It seems certain that, when evaluated in the distant perspective of history, he will be considered as one of the most influential men to appear on the world scene thus far in the twentieth century. Gandhi was basically a spiritual man. He repudiated the way of materialism and might. His ways were spiritual. His methods were spiritual. Because he used spiritual powers, India gained its freedom without a war of rebellion, of revolution. His method was freedom through non-violence.

He was a firm believer in God. When he made his historic decision to fast to gain the freedom India sought, he felt it was the will of God, it was the voice of God. Here is how he describes this decision:

"For me the voice of God, of conscience, of truth, the

inner voice or "the still small voice" means one and the same thing. I saw no form. I have never tried, for I have always believed God to be without form. But what I did hear was a voice from afar and yet quite near. It was unmistakable as some human voice definitely speaking to me, and irresistible. I was not dreaming at the time I heard the voice. The hearing of the voice was preceded by a terrific struggle within me. I listened, made certain it was the voice, and the struggle ceased. I was calm . . . .

"Could I give further evidence that it was truly the voice that I heard and that it was not an echo of my own heated imagination? I have no further evidence to convince the skeptic. He is free to say that it was all self-delusion or hallucination. It may well have been so. I can offer no proof to the contrary. But I can say this—that not the unanimous verdict of the whole world against me could shake me from the belief that what I heard was the true voice of God."

He fasted. He went to jail. He won independence for India. His methods were non-violent; they were spiritual. The methods, the way of Jesus, too, are spiritual.

The price which a man is willing to pay for his spiritual ideals is the measure of the man.

5. THE CHRISTIAN

What is the test of a Christian? We can take as our test the old proverb expressed in modern terms: The price which a man is willing to pay for the deep things of his life is the measure of the man. How true this is of the Christian. The measure of a Christian is the estimate of value, the price he is willing to pay for his Christian ideals and convictions.

The measure of a Christian is the reality and the depths of love and commitment to God as revealed in the teachings, the life and the spirit of Christ. The Christian life is well set forth in the Christian Manifesto, which we know as "The Sermon on the Mount." However, as Oliver Wendell Holmes once wrote, "Most people are willing to take the Sermon on the Mount as a flag to sail under, but few will take it as a rudder by which to steer." True Christianity is an expression of one's readiness to accept the ideals which are expressed in Jesus' revelation of God's will, and to seek the strength and courage to live by these ideals. When one lives pure Christianity in his life, he finds a deeper insight, a more compelling passion, a more vitalizing and transforming power by which to live than can be found in any other way of life.

As an illustration of a Christian consider Paul, the Apostle, who next to Jesus, shaped Christianity in its beginnings. He gave up everything for Christ. Forgetting everything else, he pressed on "toward the goal for the prize of the high calling which was in Christ Jesus, his Lord."

"What things were gain to me," he wrote, "these things I count but loss for Christ." He knew the fellowship of Christ's sufferings. "I have been crucified with Christ; it is no longer I who live, but Christ who lives in me; and the life I now live in the flesh I live by faith in the Son of God, who loved me and gave himself for me."

In order to re-enforce more vividly the measure of a Christian, let us here consider an illustration from our century. I submit one not of our own country, or even of our own way of thinking, but one of the most Christian men I have ever known, a man whose hearty cooperation and personal friendship and Christian fellowship meant much to me: Chrysostum, the Metropolitan of Smyrna, and Archbishop in the Eastern Orthodox Church.

The test of his Christian character came at the time of

the tragic destruction of Smyrna (Ismir), Asia Minor. In 1922 this city of 300,000 was destroyed by fire, with the exception of the Turkish section, and the inhabitants were forced to find refuge on the broad Quay of Smyrna, with the burning city behind them and Bay of Smyrna before them. Men of military age were taken prisoners, and the Greek population was given but a few days to leave the city. The Turkish Army had driven the Greek Army of Occupation out of Asia Minor.

Chrysostum, the Metropolitan, was summoned to the Turkish headquarters and told that he had three days to leave Smyrna, and, if at that time he had not left, he would be put to death.

The Metropolitan had found the secret of the Christian life was love to God and service to his fellow man. And when did his people need him more than now? To desert them in their tragic need would have been a repudiation of his Christian life, and a refusal of his commitment to his Christ. He could not leave the city. Rather he went about serving wherever there was need. All during those first terrible hours he could be seen moving among his people like a great saint with his long white hair and beard and long flowing black robe. Back and forth along the Quay he moved comforting his people, many dying peacefully with his sustaining arms about them.

At the end of three days he was still there serving his people. He had never thought of leaving. The Turkish soldiers arrested him. They took him to the military headquarters. When he was asked why he did not leave, his answer was: "The Good Shepherd gives his life for his sheep."

He gave his life, for a mob dragged him away and mauled him to death. It was the price he was willing to pay for his loyalty to the spirit of his Christ.

6. THE SURVIVAL OF MAN

When a new Hall of Philosophy was being erected several years ago at Harvard University, considerable consideration was given to the inscription to be placed above the entrance. The faculty of philosophy proposed the famous statement of the ancient Greeks: "Man is a measure of all things." But President Eliot made the final decision, and these were the words carved over the entrance:

> What is man that thou art mindful of him
>   and the son of man that thou dost visit him?

What is the human destiny?

It should seem evident that mankind has reached a point of progress on this planet where we must take our life and its destiny more seriously. Four recent discoveries have uprooted us from the past and revealed that our options for the future are limited.

First, the probe into space has indicated that man must remain a creature of the earth. Although space challenges man, it is very doubtful that his probings will find a better environment. Man must make the best of his home here on earth.

Secondly, our earth has a scarcity of things vital to human life. Through man's careless neglect, our air and water are becoming dangerously polluted. Vital energy resources are not inexhaustible. Yet man has been consuming these as if they were limitless.

In the third place, our minds are tortured by the thought that man has acquired the ultimate weapon of destruction. Nations have horded in arsenals an "over-kill" supply of nuclear weapons. The survival logic seems to be a mad race to produce and accumulate more.

Fourthly, even more alarming, man through his expanding knowledge is about to cross another threshold and try to play God; namely, he is beginning to manipulate human genetic material and even, perhaps, to create human beings, or, at least, to influence personality.

Never before has there been a more urgent need for human wisdom. Without it, in this dynamic age of rapid change and accelerated evolution, human life could be irreparably shattered.

At a critical period in our nation's life, James Russell Lowell wrote: "Once to every man and nation comes a moment to decide." Does our generation stand at a moment of decision? Many are agreed that we have reached the point in the progress of mankind on this planet when we must consider seriously our life and destiny on this earth. If we do not, the future is bleak and uncertain. We dare not fumble the future. It is time that we must quit playing politics, and strive for a "government of the people, by the people and for the people," when we must replace competition with cooperation, selfishness with service, enmity with friendliness, and hatred with love.

Does this seem too drastic? Vast and far-reaching changes are taking place.

Some time ago the Club of Rome, a group of industrialists and scientists, under the leadership of Aureaio Peccie, put out a challenging report expressing great concern about what is needed in this technological age if man is to have an assured future on this planet. Here is a very brief resume:

Through science and technology man has set going a worldwide process which, unless directed wisely, will upset our lives. Metaphoric changes are taking place not only in man's environment on this planet, but also in man himself. Nothing can be more important and urgent than to realize that along the road we are presently travelling, we are headed toward unseen disorder—ecological, political and social. The emergency is already upon us. The symptoms are evident—air and water pollution and other environmental changes are dangerously near to upset the delicate balanced ecology; grave social ills, such as, poverty in the midst of plenty; ever spiraling living costs and unemployment and welfare rolls; explosive relations between nations caused by distorted ideologies, selfish nationalism and racism—all these and others demonstrate a need for an extreme effort to unite all mankind in a common purpose for the welfare of all the people.

Also note what Ed. Mitchell, with keen perception, wrote after he had made the Apollo 19 journey to the Moon and back:

"Looking out of the window of the space craft at this little planet floating out there, I began to have some startling insights and feelings. It was as though all my previous philosophical questionings about a purposeful universe as opposed to a purposeless universe were suddenly resolved. I had a deep knowing that this was not just random matter floating out there, that it was a part of a divine plan, but ordered, structured, purposeful.

"But that was followed by a deep despair as I contemplated that down on earth our species seemed determined to destroy itself. We have gained a great deal of technical, objective knowledge about the physical processes of the universe, but know virtually nothing of our proper place in the universe."

Are nations to stand defeated, and the people baffled and defeated by progress? (Do not misunderstand me; I am not opposed to progress. I glory in all our scientific and technological progress.) In the midst of great progress has man forgotten his heritage, his dreams, his God? Greed grips the machine; regimentation often motivates education; corporations control the productive capacity of men to serve; nations recklessly consume the resources which the aeons have built up. Will we fumble the future?

We dare not trust the way of might and power. But

have we the capacity and the character to realize our ideals? We possess all kinds of power, but have we the wisdom to use it? We desire to have our own way so much that we cannot see God's way. We have tried to reach heaven by building upon material foundations only to see our structures crumble. We are conscious of our plight, but powerless to prevent it. We have tried to help others, but have refused the means of salvation for ourselves. We have atomic power, but are paralyzed by fear of it.

What is mankind's destiny on this planet, Earth, as it moves in its precise place in this vast cosmic order? Speaking of man, the Psalmist wrote, "Thou hast made him a little less than God." It is in God that man "lives and moves and has his being." God "binds the chains of the Pleiades, and looses the cords of Orion." Surely God holds man in His mighty keeping.

God, through the mysteries of His creativity, has given us a universe of unlimited resources of power and life. Man—heir of the ages, a part of all that has gone on before —began his long, toilsome march upward. It has been a long, long journey up the thundering, devastating centuries from the first dawn of consciousness in the mind of primitive man to the day in our generation when man stands on the plateau of the present feeling that, at long last, he has all but achieved the fulfillment of self which will release the creative powers to build the home of his dreams.

Here, at last, it seems that the human quest approaches a fusion with the cosmic process; that the spirit of man approaches the spirit of God; that there is a consciousness of the spirit in which man "lives and moves and has his being." For here now, in our generation, there has emerged a social structure through which the hard won achievements and values can be realized and passed on to the future; when the natural and the material resources of the earth can be developed and conserved; when the spiritual values and personality can be made accessible to all; when the kingdom of God can come.

Does this seem too fantastic, too labored with conceit for man to feel that, at long last, he stands on the mountaintop where he can reach out and touch the dawn of a new day which can usher in a new epoch for humanity? Nevertheless, we have dreamed that; we have hoped that; we have reason to believe that the moment of man's realization of the abundant life is at hand. God has provided this marvelous, wonderful universe adequate to man's every need.

Our generation stands either at the paradox of the centuries, or at the dawn of a new epoch for humanity. Our generation has the power to realize or to mar the dream of the ages. If it has the character, the wisdom and the faith in God, it can advance human intelligence and move on to achieve a synthesis of human intelligence and personality which will realize the spiritual. Only when this can be done, will the new day dawn.

One man dared to make this synthesis. But the imperialists and the militarists and the religionists nailed him to a cross. One day when he told the multitudes who were following him that they must also take up their cross, they turned away from following him, and he turned to his intimate friends and asked, "Will you also go away?" To which they replied, "Lord, to whom shall we go, you have the words of life."

How shall we achieve this abundant life, about which he taught, individually and collectively?

Briefly, we are creatures of this universe. We are at one with this universe. We cannot live apart from it. There is a power in this universe in which we live—God. In God we have life. God is life. Jesus taught, "God is spirit." Only when we think of Him as spirit, and only when we worship Him as spirit can we come to a fuller understanding of Him and His way.

We, all mankind, must seek to live in His spirit and in His way. God tries to make His spirit and His way known to us, but it is difficult for God to break through our self-centeredness and the heat of our desires. His spirit is ever-present with us, but we do not open up our mind to hear or our eyes to see. I know that it is difficult for us to comprehend God, or to sense the presence of his spirit. This is because communication with the divine is not determined by the audibility of God's voice, but by our willingness and our capacity to hear. Our life must be in tune with God's.

SECTION XV

THE NEW YEAR

XV. THE NEW YEAR

1. Forward With Faith
2. The Perilous Power of Choice

1. FORWARD WITH FAITH

Lo, here has been dawning another new day.
Think, wil'st thou let it slip useless away?
　Out of eternity this new day was born;
　Into eternity at night to return.
Think, wil'st thou let it slip useless away?

One New Year's Eve I listened to a radio drama. I neither recall its author nor its title, only the sketch of the drama.

It was about a very wealthy and prominent man in his community. He had, on New Year's Eve, seated himself at his desk in the library of his spacious home. He was looking over the financial pages of the evening newspaper. As he studied the reports, he thought that, if he could only know what was going to happen in the New Year ahead, he could, during the new year, clean up another fortune on the market. As he sat there in the deepening twilight of the dying year, half-thinking, half-dreaming of the idea, a voice out of the growing darkness seemed to speak: "And why not? Here are all the newspapers for every day in the coming year. Look through them if you dare."

Fearful, at first, he beheld the newspapers which contained the record of events in the year ahead; then, trembling with excitement, he turned eagerly to the news-paper for the last day of the year and scanned it through. Then continuing back through each day's newspaper, at length he came to the New Year's Day issue. As he turned to page one, immediately he read there the headlines announcing his death.

His family found him later New Year's Eve, seated at his desk in the library slumped over his desk. He had died suddenly a short time before.

What awaits us in the tomorrow? What does the New Year hold for us? Can any one speak with certainty?

Colossal changes often are taking place in our gen-eration.

What a vast mixture of tragedy and triumph, of heart-less hate and of healing love, of degradation and redemption, of dissolution and creativity! How will it all come out? Can anyone predict with certainty?

No one knows what tomorrow or the New Year will bring. This inability to peer into the future, far from being a misfortune, is a blessing. What a calamity it would be if science could create some means of predicting future events. All real zest would fall from life. Imagine, if you can, the plight of one who could know in advance every experience which would come to him, every affliction and failure, even the date of his death.

All the spirit of adventure would be taken from life. The vital element of surprise, all mystery and morality, even life itself would loose its value.

We have our hopes for enduring peace, for the welfare of our loved ones, for health, for life; but whether our hopes may be realized, God alone knows. Courageous, creative humanity, far from cringing, presses eagerly for-ward into the future with faith.

It is good for a man to come to a future which he does not know when he comes to it with faith in God. Faith and courage can sustain us in the new year. What a year of possibilities it may be! What a world in which to live! What an age in which to be alive! "Think wil'st thou let it slip useless away?"

2. THE PERILOUS POWER OF CHOICE

The power of choice distinguishes man and raises him above all other animals. Every normal human being has within him, if he will but use it, the power of choice. This power of choice is that achievement of the individual which makes almost infinite the range of the possible.

The story is told of a man, standing one evening before his window. He was looking up into the heavens where the stars were floating like lilies in a sapphire lake. He let his vision fall to the ground where he saw few more helpless beings than himself crawling toward their inevitable goal, the tomb. Already he had passed sixty of those milestones which lead to it, and he had brought nothing with him on that journey save a weakened body, a mind troubled and restless, and a life filled with sadness and remorse.

As he stood there, he recalled the time when his father had placed him, a young man, at the entrance of life's roads. One road led into a bright and happy land, whence came the sound of sweet music; the other led down into a deep, mysterious cavern where exotic and intoxicating liquid flowed instead of water. As he recalled his choice that day, anguish rose within him, and he cried out; "Oh, my youth return! Oh, my father, place me again at the entrance of life's roads that I may choose the better way."

He saw a star fall from heaven; this was a symbol of his lost youth. He saw flickering lights over the marshes; these were the symbols of the days of his lost youth. The clock in the church tower tolled off the hour of midnight;

this recalled to him his early love and the prayers that had been offered up in his behalf.

His anguish deepened, and, from the very depths of his soul, he cried out; "Oh, my heavenly Father, give me back my early days! Place me once again at the entrance to life's roads that I may choose the better way. Oh, my youth, return!" And, lo, his youth did return, for this was but a dream.

The young man challenged by his dream, arose from his bed and knelt down and thanked God that he had yet time to choose.

All you who may stand at the entrance of life's roads, know this: when the days have come and gone, and your feet stumble on the steep mountainside of life, you will call and call in vain, "Oh, my youth, return! Oh, my heavenly Father, place me again at the entrance to life's roads, that I may there choose the better way."

Today is your opportunity. You, who are young, are living in the destiny-making days of your life. You hold in your hands your own destiny, and you can make out of your life just what you will with God back of you. "Choose you this day whom you will serve." "I have set before you life and death . . . therefore choose life."

SECTION XVI

PRAYER

XVI. PRAYER

1. Prayer Is Power
2. The Voice Within the Silence
3. Teach Us to Pray

1. PRAYER IS POWER

As one drives along a U. S. highway in our town, one's attention is attracted to the many signs on either side of this thoroughfare. Most, with little modesty, seek to sell their wares. It may be a place to eat, a place to sleep, or gas galore.

Along this corridor of signs there is one which is especially intriguing. It has nothing to sell, although it could well join the others, for it too has much to offer. It is there for the men and women who think. It reads: "Prayer is Power."

Take a look at that sign and contemplate this great truth. This sign could well read, "Electricity is Power." This too is true. Electricity is a mysterious power. It is an unseen power, although there are evidences of its distribution and utilization. We really do not see electricity, but we see the manifestations of its power. With the flip of a switch it lights our homes, cooks our meals, heats our homes in winter and cools them in summer. It affords a means of communication even over long distances. With the turn of an ignition key it activates the motor in our automobile. It powers our factories and mills. What a powerful thing this unseen energy is. How manifold and useful its power. But only as we throw the switch; only as

215

we make the connection with the source, can we avail ourselves of this power. There were long centuries before man knew this power was in the universe. Now that he has come to know it and to learn the laws governing its use, the life of man has been greatly enhanced.

It is equally true, as the sign reads, "Prayer is Power." The consecrated Christian educator, the late Frank Laubach, wrote, "Prayer is the mightiest force in the world." He wrote a book using that title.

Prayer is an unseen power. While we do not see it, we can see the manifestations of its power. It is available to anyone, anytime, anywhere. He who would pray must make contact with the Source. Prayer is the means by which the spirit of man communicates with the Spirit, the Power in which all humanity lives and moves and has its being.

We marvel at the way in which the scientists in Houston have kept in communication with the men in space and on the moon. We, too, could hear and see the men at work on the moon. To the amateur, while electronic communication is a reality, nevertheless it is marvelous; it is fantastic. So also is spiritual communication. We are reminded of the words of the Astronaut on the moon, words from the 121st Psalm, "I will lift up my eyes unto the hills." The Psalm continues, "Whence cometh my help? My help comes from the Lord who made heaven and earth."

God through the unfathomable mysteries of His marvelous creativity, has given us a universe of unlimited resources of power. When we pray we league ourselves with this inexhaustible motivating power that "made heaven and earth," that rotates the earth, that holds the planets in their orbit, yes, that holds your life and holds mine. When we pray we are seeking to league ourselves with a portion of that power. When we pray we are opening up communication with God so that His wisdom and peace and power may flow into our finite mind and often into our restless and troubled soul.

Even as the instruments of electronic communication must be faultless, so also in spiritual communication. Spiritual conditions must be met. Selfishness, arrogance, pride and hatred make for poor connection with God, while honesty, integrity, humility, unselfishness and love make it possible for our communication with God to come through more clearly.

As was pointed out above with regard to what electric power can do, so we could list, from our own experience and the experiences of others, the power of prayer; yet, far better, let me point out that we shall never fully understand the power of prayer until we pray. When a man really prays, when he pours out the depths of his soul to God in prayer, when with courage and integrity he opens up his life to his Creator, ready to follow His wisdom, then he will know that God is and that He is "the rewarder of all who diligently seek Him."

Jesus prayed often. He said, men "ought always to pray." Jesus prayed at every crisis of his life. He prayed when alone in the wilderness he faced the difficult temptations of leadership. He prayed with his disciples when the religious leaders rejected him. He prayed in Gethsemane. He prayed on Calvary. Prayer made Jesus what he was. His spirit has changed the course of humanity.

Yes, "more things are wrought by prayer than this world dreams of." "Prayer is Power in all Crises."

2. THE VOICE WITHIN THE SILENCE

There are multitudes who find it hard to know what God wants them to do and be. Yet God tries to come to us. Always He tries to come, but He cannot break through our self-centeredness and the heat of our desires. We close our life to Him although He stands at the door and knocks. We close our life to Him though His light shines all about us. His spirit is evident in the world about us, but we will not open our mind to see, or our ears to hear the voice within the silence. This is because communication with the infinite is not determined by the audibility of God's voice, but by our willingness and capacity to hear. Our spirit must be in tune with His.

God is the spirit and the power in which we live. His purpose is to establish easy, intimate communication with the human spirit. He stands at the door and knocks, desiring to come in and make his abode with us. We are not shut off to a knowledge of Him gained from some seer or prophet to whom he is presumed to have spoken centuries ago. He would speak to us also. In an infinite variety of ways, He comes to us.

Out of the silence of the beauty of the earth He speaks. The beauty of the earth, the trees and the flowers, the changing seasons, the starry heavens, and through all the marvelous creativity of nature He speaks. Through illness, defeat, success, or a friendship, or the life of a little child, or the unfolding events of history—these are the language of God for all who will open up heart and mind and soul to understand.

Above all else, we may hear God through the great prophetic voices, especially through Jesus, His Beloved Son who spoke as one "having authority." He had the words of life.

Often God speaks more directly when we are in tune with His spirit. To St. Francis of Assisi God spoke through the common things of life. Leo Tolstoy came to know God and to hear Him through his sympathy for the toiling people of Russia. Mahatma Gandhi once wrote; "For me the voice of God, of conscience, of truth, of the inner voice, or 'the still small voice,' means one and the same thing." In one of his most crucial decisions, he wrote of hearing the voice of God: "What I did hear was like a voice far yet quite near . . . . I was not dreaming at the time I heard the voice. The hearing of the voice was preceded by a terrific struggle within me. I listened, made certain it was the voice, and the struggle ceased . . . . I can offer no proof. But I can say this that not the unanimous verdict of the whole world against me could shake me from the belief that what I heard was the voice of God."

What was it that induced Albert Schweitzer to go to Africa? What was it that persuaded this brilliant thinker and philosopher, this renowned musician to give up his beloved organ and his secure professorship for a scantily equipped hospital in Africa? What did he mean when he wrote that the Lord Jesus had told him to go? "He comes to us as one unknown, as of old, by the lakeside, he came to those men who knew him not. He speaks to us the same words: 'Follow Me!' and sets to us the tasks which he has to fulfill for our times. He commands. And to those who obey him, he will reveal himself in the toils, the conflicts, the sufferings which they shall pass through in his fellowship, and, as ineffable mystery, they shall learn in their own experience."

Out of the silence of her life God came to Helen Keller. She touched the lips of friends and held conversation across incredible abysses of silence. She put her wonderfully sensitive fingers to a violin and thrilled in ecstacy to its music. Helen Keller found God in the silent darkness while others missed Him in the light.

In many and mysterious ways God speaks to us. In psychic experiences, voices from within the silence come to sensitive men and women. Sometimes in dreams we are alerted and summoned to action. On one occasion— to me a never-to-be-forgotten occasion—my life was saved by a dream.

There is a river in Canada with the haunting name of "Qu'Apelle," meaning "Who calls." It takes its name from a touching Indian story. A young Indian brave set out for a distant tribe to visit the maiden whom he loved. Following a river valley, he, at night fall, wrapped his blanket about him and laid down to sleep. Late into the night he had the feeling that someone had called his name. Startled, he cried out, "Who Calls," but no answer came back. Perturbed he sank back into restless sleep. The next day, when he reached the end of his journey, he learned that his beloved had died during the night.

Ever and always through the rugged country of our life runs this river, with its mysterious and mystic call, which stirs us deep within. It may be the precious memory of a voice calling across the years which can never be recalled, or the voice of a little child, or a cry from a weary soul, or a sense within summoning us to a life of the Spirit or the gracious words of Jesus.

O living voice, within the silence calling,
    My spirit answers, wheresoe're I roam;
Through life's brief day, still keep my feet from falling,
    And lead me, through the evening shadows, home.
                                    —*Marion Han*

3. TEACH US TO PRAY
Azora Reese Mathews

A miraculous gift of our age is light. Evening comes, I flip a switch and the room is flooded with a warm glow. I cannot explain this. I only know that I stretch out my hand—and it works! Fortunately the fact that I do not understand the mechanics of these inventions does not seem to prevent my enjoying the benefits. Regardless of my lack of understanding, the fact is that it works.

So it is with prayer. I do not have to understand the mechanics of this powerful, mysterious force. I only know that, figuratively speaking, I stretch out my hand—and I am connected with this supreme Powerhouse. It works.

You will recall that the disciples asked Jesus this question: "Teach us to pray." Getting to know him they began to doubt the ostentatious prayer habits of their day. They felt that there must be a better way. In answer Jesus gave them the Lord's Prayer. This beautiful, well-organized prayer is always of value. Use it. But most of us feel the need for a more personal prayer life, too.

One of my favorite Biblical quotations are the words of the Psalmist: "When I consider thy heavens, the work of thy fingers, the moon and the stars which thou hast established, what is man that thou are mindful of him? And the son of man that thou dost care for him!" (Psalm 8:3-4) But He is—and does.

All of us are and should be overwhelmed when we contemplate God—and not with the childish conception of a bearded patriarch sitting on a throne in the sky! We are overwhelmed by this incomprehensible, mysterious, tremendous Force—Creator, Regulator, which we call God. But this is but one end of the spectrum. At the other end is the image of a loving, personal heavenly Father, slow to anger, plenteous in mercy, revealed by His Son.

Tennyson has described God as being "closer than breathing, nearer than hands and feet." Therefore, He is a part of us, within us, surrounding us. He is not far away. He is at hand, always available. We stretch out our hand and we are connected. It works!

My sweet, gentle mother developed in me at an early age a consciousness of the presence of God in my life. I grew up with the wonderful belief that here was a true Friend, ever present, always approachable. Through the years I developed what is known as "practicing the presence of God." I talked to him. It is as simple as that!

Let us liken the relationship to the enriching experience of a rare, close friendship—and how it develops. We meet someone and experience that certain "meeting of minds." We wish we could know each other better. So we pursue the acquaintanceship. It ripens into mutual trust, the sharing of confidences, problems, joys, sorrows. It is a mutual relationship, not a one-way street. We are comfortable in this relationship. We do not have to explain ourselves. We understand each other. He is as close as we want him to be. *We keep in contact*. If we thoughtlessly, or carelessly, lose contact it is our mutual loss—and our fault.

Our relationship with God develops in a similar fashion. It is a matter of growth. All powerful as He is we can approach Him in our simple way, reverencing Him, trusting Him, loving Him as He loves us. We do not have to assume a certain posture, light a candle, use formality. He is our friend. Washing dishes, walking along a busy street, lying quietly in bed before sleep comes— all are acceptable places to Him.

In an orphanage, a chaplain noted that as the boys filed into the chapel for services one lad paused for a couple of seconds and looked at the altar before taking his seat. The chaplain became curious. What could be in this boy's mind in those brief seconds? One day he said, "Jocy, I notice you stop a moment in front of the altar. What are you thinking?" He answered, "I say, 'Jesus, it's me, Joey'." He was setting up his line of communication.

So, how do I pray? My prayer life is quite informal, often spontaneous, impulsive. I rarely use the archaic terms, "thy," "thou." Occasionally they seem just right. I talk freely to Him, telling Him my problems, asking His help in solving them. I listen for the answer to my prayer —"Show me the way." But there is more to prayer than just asking. There is gratitude, appreciation, love to be expressed, and acceptance. There is the realization of the wonder and power of the Giver of Life surging within me, and I burst forth in words of love and appreciation. This is a natural impulse. Joy in a glorious sunset, a beautiful flower, a lovely day may bring forth words of deepest gratitude for the beauty of this creation which is ours to enjoy. It is wrong to take things for granted.

Another important angle in prayer is confessing our failures and asking forgiveness. This must be done in complete sincerity for we cannot fool God. Having asked, we must believe we are forgiven. To confess our faults over and over negates our appearance of trust.

Prayer is not just for times of trouble. If you went to a friend only when you needed something, the friendship would not be enriched. Neither is it a selfish project. Thus, I have a "prayer list" of certain friends whom I wish to commend for help. The list also includes leaders in our government and in world affairs. Our world is in need of a spiritual rebirth and each of us can help. For spiritual adventure has a potential that to date has only been scratched.

Why should we have to tell God our problems when He is supposed to know our very thoughts? I think this is an element of God's Psychiatry. In this honesty we should get a more enlightened view. Thus we are more receptive to the right solution He sets before us.

What about answers to our prayers? We always get an answer. But often it is not the one we want! So we wish to think it was not answered. If all our prayers were answered in our way, life would be a mess. Sometimes God says, "No!" Or "Wait!" Or, "Accept!" And sometimes we receive an answer but we misinterpret it. For we are finite creatures, living in a finite world, and perfection is only a goal, not a fact. Each of us holds within him a spark of divinity. But God also gives to each of us the right of free will. He does not force us into His patterns.

This world operates on natural laws and He does not set laws aside for us. We have barely scratched the surface in our discovery and understanding of these laws. Research of spiritual frontiers will reveal many answers to problems of disease and human relationships.

In the troubled days of 1939 King George VI, in his year-end broadcast to his people, quoted these words: "I said to the man who stood at the gate of the year: 'Give me a light that I may tread safely into the unknown.' And he replied: 'Go out into the darkness and put your hand into the hand of God. That shall be to you better than light and safer than a known way.'"*

Try it. You may creep before you walk. Spiritual development is a process of growth as surely as is physical growth, ever changing, ever maturing. Each develops his own way. You will not use all of my ideas. You will develop your own way. Just do not give up. If some day you feel utterly inadequate, just say, "Jesus, it is I." Keep the contact open. God is always there to hear.

---

*Minnie Louise Haskins

SECTION XVII

RELIGION

XVII. RELIGION

1. What Is Religion?
2. Religion Is Life
3. Man's Need For Religion
4. Religion and Solitude

1. WHAT IS RELIGION?

It has been said that it is impossible to hope for the permanency of a nation without religion to nurture it. Religion has always played an important part in the life of men and nations. Mark Hopkins once wrote, "Remove from the history of the past all those actions which have either sprung directly from the religious nature of man, or been modified by it, and you have the history of another world and another race." True religion is the foundation of the ongoing, abiding life of humanity.

What is religion? How has religion been defined? It should be defined in terms which are readily understood if it is to satisfy the longing soul of man.

My former teacher, Edward Scribner Ames, for many years the distinguished professor of philosophy in the University of Chicago, had a list of thirty-three definitions of religion. I knew a student at the university who, when writing his doctor's thesis on religion, had gathered up over a hundred definitions of religion. In fact, there is no one definition of religion; there are many, because the phases of religion are as varied as life itself. Let us look at a few definitions.

Donald Hankey said religion is "betting your life there is a God." Another of my teachers, Dean Shailer Mathews, said, "Religion is the technique by which we make available for human use the personality-producing force of the universe." Professor Ames taught that religion is the synthesis of the unrealized possibilities of life. John Dewey thought of it as the devotion to the unrealized possibilities of life. Professor Henry Witman thought of religion as a process for the realization of the most wonderful values. Professor Pratt of Harvard thought religion is the serious and social response of the person or group to that Power of Powers recognized as having influence on interests and destiny. Professor Alfred N. Whitehead of Harvard defined religion thusly: "Religion is what an individual does with his own solitariness."

Personally I have two definitions for religion. I had, like many others, been a professor of religion for a long time before I had been able to define my religion satisfactorily. While my definition is almost adequate for my thought of religion now, it may not always satisfy me. I submit my definition not as conclusive or all inclusive, but with the hope that my definition of religion will cause you to form yours.

Religion is the cooperative quest for the abundant life. And by the abundant life I mean the kind of life to which Jesus referred when he said that he came that men might have life and have it abundantly. Religion is the quest for a personal relationship and harmony with the power back of the universe, in order that through the fullest self-expression the abundant life may be gained. In more practical terms, it is the quest for the best life that one can live; it is abundant life. It is the realization of the very best that God has given to us in this universe in which we live.

2. RELIGION IS LIFE

Religion is Life. First, last and always religion is life. Religion is the whole of life. "In the beginning was the

(Word) Essence of Life, and the Essence of Life was with God, and the Essence of Life was God." (John 1:1) The purpose, the mission of Jesus as he stated it was: "I came that men might have life and have it abundantly." He did not come to give men religion nor to start a church; he came to give life.

So many people speak of religion and think of religion as if it were just a part of life, compartment, not the whole of life. They are religious when they go to church and engage in church activities. The rest of life's activities in the work-a-day world is not thought of as religious. Thus the erroneous idea grows that man's labor, his profession, his commercial, economic and political affairs are areas of life which are out of the concern of religion and are realms into which the church, since it is the institution of religion, should not enter nor project its concern.

What an erroneous concept! What an excuse for man's following his own selfishness! What false reasoning which says, "Business is business, and politics is politics, and religion is religion!" Religion is using everything for God and for the welfare of man; but many men dedicate business to their own selfishness, and politics to their desire for power, and religion is thrust aside or made a hypocritical excuse for their leisure and laziness and license.

"Vital religion," wrote Edmund Burke, "is the foundation of society, the basis on which all true civic government rests, and from which power derives its authority, laws their efficacy, and both their sanction. If it is once shaken by contempt, the whole fabric cannot be stable or lasting."

Years ago H. G. Wells expressed a basic conviction when he wrote, "Religion is the first thing and the last thing. Until a man finds God and has been found by him, he begins at no beginning and works to no end."

It was the great soul, Socrates, who said, "The end of

life is to be like unto God; and the soul following God will be like him."

All of us need to gain a new and more profound concept of what men up across the generations have called religion. We need an understanding of Jesus' redeeming, spiritually motivating interpretation of life when he said, "This is life eternal, to know thee the only true God." We have said that "God is love." He is love; but He is more than love, more than all the spiritual values which are the ways in which He expresses Himself. He is the very Essence of Life. He is Life.

Human life, as he knew it, is, in the words of wise Ben Franklin, "a preparation for life; a man is not completely born until he has passed through death." Human life is but the edge of the boundless ocean of eternity. Jesus urged men to think in the terms of the eternal. We need to acquire the power to live beyond the "terminals of the day's happenings" and, in the words of Emerson, "to hear what the centuries have to say," for some day we will merge with the Eternal. We shall live life at its best when we take Jesus seriously when he says, "I am the way, the truth and the life."

3. MAN'S NEED FOR RELIGION

In telling the story of his life the novelist Sherwood Anderson describes how a strange sensation came over him one night as he stood on a lonely road bathed in the moonlight. He writes:

"I had suddenly an odd and, to my own seeming, a ridiculous desire to abase myself before something not human; and so stepping into the moonlit road I knelt in the dust. Having no God, the gods having been taken away from me by the life about me, I kept smiling at the figure

I cut in my own eyes as I knelt in the road. There was no God in the skies, no God in myself, no conviction in myself that I had the power to believe in a God, and so I merely knelt in the dust in the silence and no words came to my lips."

Like many moderns, he believed that the impulse to worship remains, but the spirit has gone out of it. It is assumed that we cannot intellectually justify our impulse to worship now that we live in a world of science. While the psychological sciences do not come out openly against religion, they, by their explaining it, put the question in the modern minds as to the value of religion.

This questioning raises some fundamental questions: Which do we need more: a secularism which turns life into futility or a religion which gives it meaning? A disillusionment which destroys hope or a faith which inspires life with courage? A despair which leads to a resignation to meaningless fate or a trust which brings triumph over difficulties and a crusade against evil?

In fact, there is no utterly irreligious man. Many people who have abandoned formal religion are living off the good, the moral and ethical, the integrity and equity, the freedom and culture of the people who still have faith in life and maintain social integrity by that faith.

Beyond needing religion to give meaning to life, man needs it also to give him a consciousness of his oneness with humanity. It overcomes selfishness, exploitation, racial prejudice and aggression. It builds friendship, fosters brotherhood and creates love. It helps us to see life steadily and see it whole. We thus see things from the viewpoint of the personality, the spiritual, the abiding. We look at the world as we feel God sees it. From this perspective we see our own littleness, our pride, our indifference. Our hypocrisies are revealed and the inequities and injustices of our social order are set clearly before us. We need religion to really see our true self and our world about us.

Man needs religion not only to give meaning and perspective to life, but also to give a compelling moral force. Once a man really has a consciousness of his religious faith, he finds that it makes demands upon him. It surges him forward toward the common good; it impels him as with a power beyond his own.

Albert Schweitzer, driven by a divine concern for human life, left the university and the comforts of civilization to build a hospital in the wilds of Africa and to save the people from their diseases. All about us are men and women who, possessed by an ideal, are giving themselves in service to others. Everywhere you see a great personality you see one with an understanding of life's meaning and an urgency to make that meaning enhance the life of others.

Take religion away and life is robbed of much of its meaning, its perspective and its compelling moral force. The impulse to worship may remain but the shrine is in ruin. Robbed of religion, we may end where we began, with a picture of a man who had an odd, a ridiculous desire to abase himself before something not human, a man kneeling in the dust of the road in the moonlight, with no God above him, no God within him, no conviction that he had even the power to believe in a God; so he merely kneels in the dust with no words of gratitude on his lips. "The fool," wrote the Psalmist, "said in his heart there is no God."

> I sought his love in sun and stars,
>   And where the wild seas roll,
> And found it not. As mute I stood,
>   Fear overwhelmed my soul;
> But when I gave to one in need,
> I found the Lord of Love indeed.

I sought his love in lore of books,
    In charts of science' skill;
They left me orphaned as before—
    His love eluded still;
Then in despair I breathed a prayer
The Lord of Love was standing there!
            —*Thomas Curtis Clarke*

4. RELIGION AND SOLITUDE

One of the most profound words uttered about religion in our generation was from Alfred N. Whitehead, mathematician and philosopher of Harvard. "Religion is what one does with his solitude."

Jesus certainly knew what to do with his solitude. We read in the gospels about how Jesus went off into a solitary place to pray. We read about his having spent the night in prayer. At every time of ebbing strength, at every important decision in his life, he sought the silence and solitude to find the resources of power. These retreats always resulted in a restoration of strength and power for Jesus. Out of these he came with power, poise and peace, the master of himself and of men. He could completely lose himself in the mystical presence of God. He emerged with a clearer vision of God's will and purpose.

A few others have been able at times to find this oneness with God. Paul, the Apostle, saw his heavenly vision. Plotinus, the Alexandrian mystic, had his heavenly visions. Mohammed tells of how he was "caught up into heaven." St. Francis, George Fox, Joan of Arc, and a host of others heard the "still small voice." Abraham Lincoln sought God in solitude in our nation's most crucial time. Gandhi, through silence and disciplined meditation, found the way to lead a subcontinent of over three hundred million people in a nonviolent revolution to freedom.

Great men with great calls and commissions have passed through times—hours, days, months—when their deepest convictions were put to the severest tests. Often the very validity of their cause was at stake. In these tremendous conflicts alone with God, they gained clarity of purpose and strength. In solitude of such prayers, the world's great religious truths have been born. Out on the hills of Nazareth, out in the wilderness of Judea, out in the heavy solitude and seclusion of the night came Jesus' personal religion. Silence, seclusion and solitude made Jesus what he was and always will be to men. "To go up into the mountain," suggests Evelyn Underhill, "and return an ambassador of God to men, this has always been the way of humanity's greatest friends."

Into the deepening gloom of Gethsemane, Jesus went to learn more clearly whether his vision of God was true. He did not want to face rejection and death. He prayed in agony, "Not my will but thy will be done." He prayed until there came a certainty of God's will, until from the Source he had drawn the strength and courage which has challenged and inspired men.

"This prayer on the Mount of Olives," wrote the philosopher, Hoffding, "is the highest moment in the history of prayer, the most profound word in religion ever uttered."

Here is an untapped source of power to all who will turn to it. The most valuable moments in our life could be those spent in quiet and in solitude seeking oneness with the power in which we live and move and have our being.

> Let thy soul walk slowly in thee,
>   As a saint in heaven unshod,
> For to be alone with Silence
>   Is to be alone with God.
>   —*S. M. Hageman*

SECTION XVIII

THE SPIRITUAL

XVIII. THE SPIRITUAL

1. The Quest For Spiritual Power
2. The Primacy of the Spiritual
3. Adventuring Into Outer and Inner Space
4. Man's Inner Resources of Power
5. How the Spiritual Enhances Life

1. THE QUEST FOR SPIRITUAL POWER

Every man and woman with ideals wants to live life at its best. Religion affords them a way to life's best. It is in God that all humanity "lives and moves and has its being."

In the more difficult times of our life we need a strength that is greater than our own to see us through. Confused and distracted by worries and responsibilities and the confusion of our troubled times, men and women, young and old, need time for silence, for quiet meditation and for reflection upon and harmony with life's fundamental values. They need to wait in some "upper room" for power which comes through fellowship with the eternal God. In this fast-moving, dynamic world of ours we need this fellowship as never before.

In this quest for power, not ruthless power, nor personal power, but spiritual power, a power that will sustain our life at its best, what in all this world is comparable to the power of religion? "Thou wilt keep him in perfect peace whose mind is stayed on Thee." Yes! " Though I walk through the valley of the shadow of death, I will fear no evil, for thou art with me." "I can do all things through Christ who strengtheneth me." "Thou has made us for thyself, and our hearts are restless until they rest in thee." "There is an enduring power, not ourselves, which makes for righteousness." Such has been the significant testimony of generation after generation of those who have turned to religion for the strength with which to live. "They that wait upon the Lord shall renew their strength," is a truth which has stood the test of time.

Jesus always left the impression that in working with God he had at his command energies not possessed by those about him. "He went forth in the power of the spirit into Galilee." This same power, he taught, is accessible to all who, in questing for it, are willing to pay the price. "If any man will come after me let him deny himself and take up his cross daily and follow me." "He that believes on me, the works that I do he shall do also, and greater works than these shall he do." "The water that I shall give . . . shall be a spring of water bubbling up for eternal life." "If you have faith . . . you can remove mountains." The life of Jesus is replete with assurances of the availability of this spiritual power to all who seek fellowship with God.

What Christian men and women need today is somehow to grasp that which released in Jesus and his disciples this spiritual power. We have not been following closely Jesus' way nor heeding his emphases upon spiritual values. In our times men have been plying their energy and intellect to the understanding and mastery of the material forces of life. Untold resources of physical power have been released. Marvelous techniques for its control are now in the hands of man. Every year adds to the scientific knowledge of material powers which significantly transform our life. While much of this is good and should not be halted, nevertheless, man is now awakening to a realization that these material powers may end in his tragic destruction. Yet, they could become a source for more abundant life. The direction is yet to be determined by whether we shall release sufficient spiritual power to humanize and spiritualize the material powers.

This will come about only when Christians fully recognize that humanity's life will rise to its best when undergirded by spiritual values.

2. THE PRIMACY OF THE SPIRITUAL

Jesus always thought of and spoke of God as Spirit. "God is Spirit." This concept of God is a most significant contribution to life. It is in the Spirit that men live. What is its meaning and significance? It cannot be dismissed carelessly.

Our age has engaged its energies and its intellect in exploring the natural, the material resources of our earth. We have emphasized the material, the practical and the scientific, and we have achieved vast wealth and great power. Much of this has been good and has enhanced the life of man. Unfortunately, the ultimate realities have been neglected. The development of the spiritual has not kept pace with the material. We have greatly ignored the vast yet latent spiritual resources. Techniques in the natural and material interest us more than creative purpose and meaning.

Our age has a passionate hunger for power and possessions, and we have obtained these in great abundance. But who can tell what vast spiritual resources will be amassed when the same diligent and scientific effort is spent in the realization of an equal spiritual hunger. We have attained great scientific control over our physical world and exploited the resources of our planet. We have used these very largely for power and possessions and exploited them often thoughtlessly, recklessly, even ruthlessly, and at times, to our undoing.

More than $20 billion has been spent in landing men on the moon and in the exploration of outer space. All this has been for the good. Now we must be willing to spend like sums on the exploration of the inner space of man. When we think of the limits of man's physical reach into outer space, we realize the challenge of the exploration into the infinite range of the mind of man. There are vast mysteries in the psychic realm of humanity to be explored. These challenging scientific mysteries in the yet unexplored spiritual realms are awaiting the heroism of a Columbus or the adventures of an astronaut, for here lie the mysteries of life.

We have life. But whence did it come? Whither does it go? What and where is the Essence of Life, the power in which man lives and moves and has his being? What is the ultimate reality? What is truth?

Back across the centuries we can see towering personalities rising up from the multitudes: Moses, Confucius, Buddha, Jesus, Augustine, Francis of Assisi, Luther, Lincoln, Gandhi, Pope John XXIII and others. What were the spiritual powers possessed by these personalities? For example, whence the spiritual and psychic powers possessed by Jesus, powers by which he did many wonderful things which baffled the understanding of others, powers which made him what he was and is? Modern psychology is groping wistfully for an understanding of the laws of the psychic realm.

Again, what are the powers possessed by a few among us who see visions and hear words the rest of us do not see or hear? To the rest of us their communications are fantastic. But we must believe them for they are men and women of integrity. We cannot write off the psychic realities of life. Its challenge must be met.

Multitudes of people pray. Other multitudes, when they get into a tight spot, turn to prayer. There is the psychologist who came to feel no need for God and prayer. Then, his child became deathly sick and, as he stated it, "I came bawling back to God."

Many attest to the value of prayer. Tennyson wrote, "More things are wrought by prayer than this world dreams of." Frank Laubach wrote, "Prayer is the mightiest force in the world."

What is prayer? What are the psychic and spiritual laws governing it? We should heed the advice of Charles Steinmetz, the late electrical wizard, when he advised that there be established laboratories for the study of God and prayer.

How we long to know more of the Essence of Life, about God! How we long to know more about ourselves! How we long to know more about the spiritual powers possessed by Jesus! What really happened in the Upper Room in Jerusalem on that Pentecost long ago? Something happened which changed the course of human history. Surely, the human mind will quest until it finds a satisfying answer.

The infinite range of the human mind—here is man's great and adventurous challenge. We are just beginning to realize that there are lying latent within the human personality spiritual powers only awaiting release in order to spring forth into the realization of life beyond the dreams of man. These spiritual powers are subject to the same orderly cosmic processes as are the physical forces. The approach to an understanding of them will come as man discovers their basic laws and learns how to obey them.

In the Spirit of God, the Essence of Life, lie the resources for a rewarding and worthy destiny of man.

3. ADVENTURING INTO OUTER AND INNER SPACE

Gigantic strides are being taken in the exploration of outer space. To the average person the accomplishments seem fantastic. But to the space scientist who works and thinks day after day in the laboratories and research centers, the "fantastic" becomes an accomplished reality. The scientist knows and feels that this is only the beginning, that greater achievements lie ahead. But only as they discover more of the cosmic laws and learn how to manipulate them, will progress be made. Because we live in a cosmos, not amid chaos, man, through the knowledge of cosmic laws, moves out and on into outer space.

Who, in my generation, a few years ago, ever thought that man would ever reach the moon? Because men have had faith in the physical and natural laws, they now, after long research, experimentation, and testing of accumulated knowledge of these laws, launch out into outer space and send men to the moon.

Not only have "fantastic" advances been made in the realm of outer space; but, also, the jet-like pace of advance of scientific and technological knowledge is speeding mankind on to the threshold of a future beyond the dreams of men. Through the advances in medical science, once dreaded diseases have been abolished. Through advances in electronics, computers and cybernetics, accumulated knowledge has been put at man's fingertips. But awesome as all this seems it is matched by man's infinitely ranging mind.

All this challenges us anew and with greater insistency with the age-old question: "Can man by searching find God?" We have made great strides forward toward the conquest of outer space, but what of the inner space of man?

Here, indeed, may lie the realm of man's greatest and rewarding and supreme accomplishments. Fantastic as have been our discoveries and accomplishments in our physical and natural realms, they could well sink into insignificance in comparison to the explorations into man's infinitely ranging mind. Psychology and psychic research have not even begun to scratch the surface. All too often this realm has been left to the amateur. Where chemistry and physics were a century or two ago left in the hands of the alchemist, and outer space to the astrologer, so the inner life, the spiritual, has yet to be studied by the careful methods of scientific research. Too often, so-called "spiritualists" have monopolized the attention given to the spiritual resources of the human personality.

Only when man comes to the recognition of the values and possibilities of life's spiritual resources, and only as he applies to their study the same scientific method and research will he begin to acquire knowledge and make progress in the inner life such as he had made in the outer space.

Here may be the next great adventurous task for the Christian Church—at least for dedicated Christians. Should not the Church lead in the research of man's soul? The many projects carried on by the Church for man's physical and social well-being are highly commendable and should be increased, but "what will it profit a man if he gain the whole world and lose his soul?" Let the Church also set up its laboratories and centers for research into the yet unreached resources of the spiritual life. We would do well to heed the words of the great electrical wizard, the late Charles Steinmetz: "When men understand the spiritual power in the universe and gear into it, life will change for the better and move forward at a prodigious rate." To this we can add the words of another great thinker: "It does not yet appear what we shall be."

4. MAN'S INNER RESOURCES OF POWER

While in New York City, I had an afternoon visit with a long-time friend. We have had many common interests across the years. This day our conversation centered about the importance of the spiritual in life. We both have given much thought to this, but from very different angles. In fact, we both have written books on this subject. But these, also, express our differing approaches. (The title of his book is *A Life After Death*,* mine is *A Quest for Life*.**) He related to me this day some of the deep spiritual and psychic experiences he had had. After a time, I broke in to say, "These are fantastic." "Of course, they are fantastic," he replied. "They are fantastic to those who have never had such experiences."

Down across the centuries deeply mystical souls, like St. Paul, have had their "heavenly vision." St. Francis heard sounds which others' ears could not hear. Plutonius saw visions which others' eyes could not see. So, also, Swedenborg, John Bunyan and a host of other mystics have had strange and unusual spiritual and psychic experiences which, viewed realistically, strain our credulity.

We cannot pass over lightly nor dismiss these as magic. Neither can we ignore them as utterly fantastic, much less leave them to be exploited by the unintelligent.

It is not easy to probe deeply into the inner reaches of the human mind, or to analyze the spiritual resources which well up out of that mind and soul, and which create spiritual values and powers. There are many powerful spiritual values; such as truth, integrity, kindness, meekness, friendship and love. These and other spiritual things cannot be seen or cannot be analyzed in a laboratory; nor can prayer or spiritual experience be tested as you would test or analyze your garden soil. New methods of testing and analysis must be developed to study the spiritual realm of life. Research centers need to be set up. Certainly no adequate, methodical, scientific approach has been

*S. Ralph Harlow by Doubleday & Co.
**Christopher Publishing House

organized (save that undertaken by J. B. Rhine of Duke University) to explore the deep inner phenomena of man's mind and spirit. In this neglect man could well be losing the most dynamic and destiny determining power in the world.

In our material realm the atom, after millions of dollars in research and years in experimentation by top scientists, has come out of physical laboratories as the greatest source of modern material power. Love is doubtless the greatest of spiritual powers, but it cannot be split into parts, nor produced in a laboratory. It wells up out of the deep inner spirit of a human personality. It is a part of the whole creative spirit of the universe. It can become man's greatest and most helpful source of power.

Nuclear power could destroy our earth. Spiritual power, if we can yet fully discover and realize it, can transform our world.

5. HOW THE SPIRITUAL ENHANCES LIFE

Within Life's spiritual resources there are powers which can enhance any life. They are accessible to all who league themselves to them and undertake their disciplines. Where they are cultivated and applied through disciplines of mind and emotions, of personality and character, and of the spirit through silence and meditation and prayer, life—individual and social—is greatly enlightened and enhanced. What happens, it would seem to be, is that one's faculties are alerted and more sensitive. The mind works more clearly and logically; the heart grows more responsive. The whole being acts and re-acts more swiftly and more surely; the conscience becomes more discerning and authoritative. Things are seen more vividly; speech is uttered with greater integrity and more assurance. One is motivated with greater confidence and courage. The whole person becomes more creative and adventuresome. The surge of power within enables one to organize and utilize latent and unrealized resources, to raise the character to its fullest stature, and to create the personality God most desires one to have.

Jesus possessed spiritual power, and he did many wonderful things. How did he do these? How did he have the power to do what he did? He leagued himself to God, and God to Jesus is spirit. He availed himself of the spiritual resources. He drew from the source of power. So completely did he league himself with God that he could say, "I and the Father are one." He worked the work of God. "The Father works and I work." He assured his followers that those who had faith in his way will do "the work which I do, and greater works than these will he do."

He further assured them that, if they followed God's way, nothing would be impossible for them. He stated it thus: "With men it is impossible but with God (working with God) all things are possible." There are no limits to the human personality and to human destiny when men learn and follow the way of the spirit, the laws of the eternal God, and "God is spirit."

Contemplate for some time these wonderful lines by Bishop Trench:

> Lord, what a change within us one short hour
> Spent in Thy presence will avail to make!
> What heavy burdens from our bosoms take,
> What parched grounds refresh as with a shower!
> We kneel, and all around us seems to lower;
> We rise, and all, the distant and the near,
> Stands forth in sunny outline brave and clear.
> We kneel, how weak! We rise, how full of power!
> Why, therefore, should we do ourselves this wrong,
> Or others, that we are not always strong.

SECTION XIX

SUFFERING

XIX. SUFFERING

1. The Fellowship of Suffering
2. When Sorrow Comes
3. Why Suffering?
4. What to Do About Suffering
5. When Suffering Persists

1. THE FELLOWSHIP OF SUFFERING

Thornton Wilder wrote a three-minute play drawn against the background of the pool of Bethesda in Jerusalem. The play engages three characters: the angel who troubled the waters at the pool; a man just emerging from the pool, having been healed; the third, a doctor, infirm all his life, who rails bitterly because he never chanced to be at the pool when the waters were troubled. "Why," he asked the angel, "could I not be plunged beneath the waters and be cleansed?" The angel tells him why: "Had you been healed, you could not heal."

Those who have experienced suffering themselves can more fully understand the suffering of others. Many may try to understand the suffering of body and soul in others, they may try to give sympathy and strength and courage, but only those who have felt the aching loneliness of suffering themselves can fully understand the suffering of others. It has always been so.

In the fourth century, St. Augustine fell into deep mental anguish; but, out of his suffering, he became the century's great saint, bringing sustaining faith in a time of great despair. St. Francis, in the twelfth century, reared in wealth and luxury, tossed on a bed of sickness, crying out against his pain; but out of that anguish surrendered all claim to fortune, abandoned luxury, and became such an instrument of God's peace that, with thirteen young men, he brought Italy nearer to the spirit of Jesus. Dostoevsky, a man who lived his entire life under the handicap of a disturbing disease, suffered excessively from feelings of inferiority and inadequacy. He spent several years in Siberia, a political prisoner. But in him dwelt a spirit of compassion for his fellow sufferers. No other Russian has ever spoken to suffering humanity as he spoke through his novels. These and a host of others, through suffering, have taken compassion on others. Pain and sorrow accepted will give us an understanding of others in times of their suffering and sorrow.

We, too, may let pain, suffering and sorrow become the refining tools of our character. All about us today are pain, suffering and hearts that sorrow. To meet these helpfully demands sympathetic understanding. All who suffer are so closely related that they enter into a fellowship of suffering. Out of this fellowship can come strength and courage to others who are baffled and fearful in their efforts to understand the fuller meaning of life's deeper and more trying experiences. If it were not that we were all bound together in a human fellowship, doubtless no one of us would be able to face the griefs, the sufferings, the loneliness, the frustrations and the denials of hope which so often baffle life.

You suffer, yes. And I suffer, too. And if I see how courageously you are bearing your suffering, I am ashamed of my weakness in bearing mine. You have deep sorrow, yes. And I have known sorrow, too; and, if I see how gallantly you bear your sorrow, I am reproached for my stubbornness if I am unwilling to accept mine. It is your way of meeting your grief and sorrow that gives me the courage and the will to meet mine. It is your kind concern for the needs of others that challenges me for an understanding of others in their suffering and sorrow.

It is this fact that some men and women go so bravely down into the valley of the shadow of death only to come out with the light of faith expressed more radiantly in their life—it is this fact that gives the rest of us the courage to walk more firmly in faith and hope. This awakening of the moral and spiritual courage that is in every soul is the most helpful therapeutic for grief and sorrow.

In the early days of my ministry I found it most difficult to minister to men and women in grief and sorrow. How inadequate I felt, until I learned that the truest help which we can render to those afflicted in grief is not to take the burden away, but to call out their best strength that they may be able to bear the burden more bravely. For a burden well borne is better than a burden removed. It gives a person sympathetic understanding which moves him to help bear another's burden.

How beautiful and how radiant is the life of one who has known a deep sorrow, and who, out of sympathetic understanding, can evoke a gallantry of spirit which can draw other sufferers into that glorious fellowship of those who, by bearing their own cross courageously, have contributed to others a new faith, a greater courage and an abiding hope. This fellowship seeks

To comfort all who mourn,
to give a garland instead of ashes,
the oil of gladness instead of mourning,
the mantle of praise instead of a faint spirit.
                                        —*Isaiah 61-3*
A Prayer for a Friend—

"Dear Lord make me an instrument of Thy peace in the heart of my friend; where there is turmoil, may I bring peace; where there is sadness, happiness; where there is narrowness of disappointment, a wideness of vision; where there is pain, the balm of understanding."

2. WHEN SORROW COMES

Death is universal. It is inevitably a part of life. But it is also a part of God's plan that He lead us into a fuller understanding which can help us make readjustments, and which can give strength for our weakness and comfort for our sorrow. Death will always remain a journey into the unknown, but a journey with hope and faith—an entrance into a "house of many mansions."

The Christian should and can be prepared to understand death. Our Christian faith teaches us that death is not the end of life, but the beginning of another. Life is eternal. As to the mystery of the details of life after death, that is what makes it "life's greatest adventure." Every thing in our universe, the very trend of the universe, indicates that the great creative power, God, has so designed things that, whatever may happen, life goes on.

When sorrow comes with the death of a loved one, it brings a feeling of deep loss. Grief is inevitable. Even Jesus wept at the tomb of a friend. Grief sweeps over all of us. It is harmful to repress it with false bravery. It is better to let it be expressed sincerely and unaffectedly. When sorrow is deep and the feeling of loss is great, we find it hard to think of anything else. This may even become a wholesome experience. One can live with an unseen presence. This need not be morbid. It can become a deep, spiritual experience. Although our grief may be beyond words to express, we can adjust our life to it. We must realize that countless others have adjusted themselves, and, with courage and faith, we can also.

When sorrow comes with the death of one we love, there inevitably arises within us a feeling of guilt. Psychologists have pointed out that most of us in sorrow experience excessive feelings of guilt. We chastise ourselves by wondering what more we could have done, how we could

have been more helpful, more appreciative, more understanding, more loving. These feelings come accusingly to
us.   If they are not fully understood as normal and
common, they can hang over us like a cloud to the end of
our days. We cannot escape them, but we can understand
them.

Regardless of how we may try to rationalize our sorrow
and grief, the parting with one we dearly love brings pangs
of earthly separation.   There sweeps over us an aching
loneliness of soul. How often, when a husband and wife
who have lived in close and loving companionship are
separated by death, the one left behind is wrapped in utter
loneliness.   Some of you, dear readers, have experienced
this, and those who have not might well enter into sympathetic understanding with those who have. So often
there comes the feeling that the one who has passed on is
away only for a short time and will soon be returning; but
no, an awareness of loneliness returns. There is a jouney
which must be taken alone.   There are questions which
forever must remain unanswered, there is information
which never again can be had, there is appreciation which
never again can be expressed, there are kindnesses which
never again can be shared. Often there comes momentarily
the impulse to share the first rose from the garden, the
first fruit from the orchard, some good news received, or a
sadness which now must be borne alone. There is a heart
that is as empty as a house.

In one of my pastorates I knew well a very fine couple.
After a long illness the husband passed on. Following the
funeral, as I visited the widow on several occasions, I
found her grief, while not bitter, was very deep.   Her
constantly repeated wish was that she might soon join
her departed husband. This wish deepened pathetically
with the passing time. It became increasingly so over the
next eighteen years in which she survived him, and those

were years of sadness. Also, I remember the Church School teacher who lost her husband in the prime of life. Later she wrote me, "Even after thirteen years, the loneliness seems too difficult to bear."

It is difficult for many to accept death. No logic can assuage the broken heart. It wants comfort and peace. It wants to turn back, to recall the life that has gone—this cannot be.

The years of loneliness need not be years of sadness as illustrated by a member of another church I served who lost his wife. Theirs had been a beautiful companionship. The separation could have been most grievous. His life could have been filled with utter loneliness. But he wrote recently: "Death is not the end but the beginning. It is a step upward in our heavenly Father's plan. Loneliness has been replaced by precious memories of wonderful years together and of the life that is yet to be." These "precious memories" have filled his life with a new radiance. He has been spending his remaining years in helpfulness to others.

Of course, there will be the sense of sorrow in the death of a loved one. It will remain with us as long as life lasts. However, the anguish, the grief and the aching loneliness can be transcended by "precious memories," memories of journeys across the years, memories of living and working together, of carefree vacations, of evenings watching the sunset over the lake, of hearing the laughter of the children at play, of sitting under the mystery of the stars, and of venturing together in common tasks amid the stress and strain of the busy world and reaching out toward the ultimate goal. These can become an unfailing source of life and joy and love rather than what might otherwise be heart-breaking loneliness.

While it is so true that "every man shall bear his own burden," we should seek to "bear one another's burdens."

When burdens seem too heavy to bear, the most helpful suggestion is, to use the old phrase. "Cast your cares on the Lord and he will care for you." When we do our best and then place our trust in God, God gives us the inner resources of strength and courage to carry on. Strength and courageous living do come to those who can make the full surrender to God. If we can do this, experience has convinced me, God will assume much responsibility for us. As the Apostle Paul, in his second letter to the Corinthians wrote:

"Blessed be God, even the Father of our Lord Jesus Christ, the Father of all mercies, and the God of all comfort, who comforts us in all our tribulation, that we may be able to comfort them which are in any trouble, by the comfort wherewith we ourselves are comforted by God."

In God we shall find the strength, the courage, and the endurance we need. He may not always be able to rid us of our pain and suffering and sorrow; but He gives us, moment by moment, the strength and courage to see it through. He sustains us by His spirit. Even, if we face death, God assumes responsibility for leading us into a new life beyond this. Even though we "take the wings of the morning, and dwell in the uttermost parts of the sea; even there thy hand shall lead me, and thy right hand shall hold me. If I say, Surely the darkness shall cover me, even the night shall be light about me." (Ps. 139) When, in faith, we have given our life over to His keeping, we can confidently commend to Him our spirit.

Such a trust in God can relieve our life of anxiety; but it does more: It brings a serenity, a calm and a confidence in the Power in which we live.

> The Power that holds the planets in their courses,
>   That places limits on the restless sea,
> Holds my life within its mighty keeping—
>   Always holds me.

I say this over and over when the storms are heavy,
   I say it when the night is on the land;
I whisper that behind the Power Almighty
   Is God's kind hand.

And so I rest as a swan rests on a river—
   Quiet and calm amid life's troubled flow;
I know I am held by a power and a love that never
   Will let me go.

—Grace Noll Crowell

A Prayer— Gracious and loving God increase our wisdom
         and our understanding that the Power
         that places limits on the restless sea,
         that guides the astronauts in their orbit
         that holds the planets in their course,
             Holds our life too within its mighty keeping,
         Thou Power Divine.

3. WHY SUFFERING?

What shall we think of all the suffering in our world?
What can we do about it? The long ages of man have been
filled with suffering. Suffering has been caused by the
ravages of nature, hunger, disease and war. In the long
journey of man up it has been said, "Man's life is of few
days and full of woe." Our generation has had its full
share of suffering.

In my youth we saw the sufferings caused by the cruelties of World War I. And, as if the cruelties of war were
not enough, many homes suffered physically and mentally
from the great "flu" epidemic which took its deadly toll
from homes by the thousands. But the sufferings of World
War I were small in comparison with the sufferings so

widespread by World War II, with its reeking retinue of
destruction, disease and death. Unwittingly we allowed
ourselves to be dragged into the irrational and frustrating
war in Southeast Asia which we now so deeply regret. If
war continues to be the lot of mankind, may God have
mercy on us; it could bring to man more suffering than he
could endure.

Suffering does not mean much to us when we are far
removed from it. In spite of its agonies most of us go on
undisturbed. Untouched by it we tend to ignore it. We
go to bed to restful sleep and arise the next morning
refreshed to go about our work. Regrettably many among
us are engaged in planning and making instruments capable
of more devastating suffering.

It is when suffering comes home to us that we feel its
anguish and sorrow. We are baffled when we see the good
and the innocent suffer, especially if they are near and
dear to us. There are those of us who have felt the aching
anguish as helplessly we see a loving companion, whose life
is the very essence of good, and who has lived mostly for
others, suffer from a distressing sickness for which the
scientists, as yet, have no cure.

Often the questions perplex us. Why should the good
and the innocent suffer? Why all this pain and suffering?
These are questions which man has been asking up across
the ages. Perhaps man will go on asking them forever.

While we may not find a satisfying answer for suffering,
there is something we can do about it. We can work to
find ways to remove the causes of suffering. We can dedicate our efforts to the removing of the causes of war and
to the bringing of peace that there may come peace on
earth and good will among men. We can cease to glorify
war; we can extol peace. Many courageous souls are already
committed to this effort. When more of us join with them,
we can more effectively devote our labors, our skills and

our resources to the conquest of hunger, disease and pain.
In many laboratories scientists, physicians and psychiatrists are carrying on research into the ills of humanity.
Already, in many areas, their efforts have been gloriously
rewarded.

If men could only learn to live on this earth in peace
and good will, the billions and billions in money and the
abundant resources of our planet could be turned away
from man's inhumanity to man toward the enhancement
of our common humanity. Man's common task should be
devoted to the creation of a better life for all mankind
physically, morally and spiritually. Any other work is
unworthy of man.

4. WHAT TO DO ABOUT SUFFERING

Since the dawn of time humanity has been haunted by
the problem of suffering. Age after age men and women,
in the face of trouble and suffering in life, have turned
again and again to seek an answer which would be satisfying to their soul. One of the oldest Hebrew books, the
book of Job, deals with this problem of suffering. The
ancient Greeks sought for a solution. This problem con-
stitutes the background of the philosophy of Buddhism.
Religious teachers and philosophers of the ages have grap-
pled with it, but have found no satisfying answer. Still
men and women ask the question: "Why does not God do
something about suffering?"

Basically this question makes the wrong approach.
God does not cause suffering, nor does He send trouble.
Most trouble comes through man's failure, man's ignorance,
man's hatred, man's disobedience and lack of harmony
with the laws of life. Man lives in a law abiding universe.
Man cannot break these laws. When man, willfully or in

ignorance, disregards these laws, he suffers and causes others to suffer. As long as man has the freedom of choice, or until man fully understands and harmonizes with the physical, the moral and the spiritual laws of the universe, there will be suffering.

Therefore, rather than asking the question: "Why does not God do something about suffering and the evil which causes it?" the more intelligent question must be: "Why does not man do something about suffering and evil?" It is man who must do something about suffering and about the evils which cause suffering. Only with this approach will a solution be possible for the problem of evil.

An English theologian, L. P. Jacks, has suggested to us that there is a way in which to think more clearly about the problem of suffering and evil. It is by strengthening one's will to oppose evil whenever and wherever it appears. Think of evil as that which demands our greatest opposition. Never for a moment in your life allow yourself to tolerate evil. Determine to oppose it. Think of the treachery of Judas as a crime which three thousand times thirty pieces of silver would never induce you to perpetrate against the most debased of your fellow men. Think of the hunger, the disease and the ignorance of the under-privileged people as such an untenable condition that it demands the utmost effort to eradicate. Think of war with all its agonies, its harrowing memories, and its reeking retinue of hatred, suffering and death as something which must never occur again, and against which you will strive with all your energy and your intelligence that it may never happen again.

Have you ever suffered? Have you ever felt the cruel crushing sting of evil? Would you think more clearly about it? Then look about you and see all the suffering and agony and evil in the world and, wherever you see it, work, and never grow weary, that there may be an end to it.   With this approach to the problem of suffering, we shall begin to enter into a closer relation and harmony with the way of the eternal God.

5. WHEN SUFFERING PERSISTS

I shall yet praise him, who is the health
of my countenance, and my God.
                                          Psalm 42:11

When suffering persists, when trouble overwhelms, when distress exists, when pain seems unendurable, what can we do?   Experience has persuaded me that strength and courage come through a complete commitment to the Power in which we live, to a supreme surrender to God.

Many, many others have come to this same place in life. Job reached this conclusion. Jesus, out of the agony of the Garden of Gethsemane, had reached the place where he could say, "Thy will be done," and with quiet and confidence he endured to the end. This commitment brings a "peace which passes understanding."   It is this trust and confidence in God that is so fundamental to life.

Thus we come to a more satisfying understanding of all the suffering, the pain and even the evil in the world. We feel with others that we are forced back to the conclusion of the Book of Job: the problem of suffering is insoluble. We may never find a satisfying answer, yet there is something infinitely more important to us than a complete understanding of this, one of life's most baffling questions. That something is an unfaltering trust in the power, the wisdom and the love back of this universe in which we live, no matter how baffling, how disturbing, how perplexing the vicissitudes of life. The man or woman who has passed through the agony of dark hours, and who has worked his or her way through to a realization of an unfaltering trust in God, has found peace, a peace which leads life to triumph and victory. How beautiful in life are the men and women who have come up out of the Valley of the Shadow of Death with the light of faith and trust burning more brightly in their lives.

In the deep resources of religion lie the strength and the courage to live through life's most difficult days. Von Hegel, the German philosopher, has written: "Christianity has not explained suffering and evil; no one has done so, no one can do so. Yet Christianity has done two things greater, more powerful and profitable for us. Christianity has, from the first, immensely deepened and widened—the fact, the reality and the awful potency and baffling mystery of sorrow, pain, sin—things which abide with men across the ages. And Christianity has, from the first immensely increased the capacity, the wondrous secret and force, which issues in practical living, loving, transcending utilization, transformations of sorrow and pain and even sin. Christianity gave to souls the faith and the strength to grasp life's nettles."

This is what we need, and this is what God gives: strength to grapple with life's perplexities.

SECTION XX

TRIUMPHANT LIVING

XX. TRIUMPHANT LIVING

1. The Eternal Choice
2. The Measure of Greatness
3. Turning Life's Defeats into Victories
4. Good Men Who Have Failed
5. Where There Is No Defeat

1. THE ETERNAL CHOICE

When Solomon became King of Israel, he dreamed that God came to him and said: "Ask what I shall give you." And Solomon in his dream answered out of what was in his thoughts: "Give thy servant an understanding heart to judge thy people, that I may discern good and bad." He had realized the difficulty of the eternal choice between good and bad.

This age-old choice continues to baffle us. Good and bad do not always appear in white and black. There are many shades of light and darkness. The varying shades of gray make it difficult to distinguish good and evil. So, here, while we have no pat answer to give, some suggestions may be helpful.

A generation ago, Conte du Nouy, in his helpful book *Human Destiny*, makes this distinction between good and evil when he states, "Good is that which contributes to the course of ascending evolution and leads us away from the animal toward freedom. Evil is that which opposes evolution and escapes it by regressing toward ancestral bondage, toward the beast. In other words, from a strictly human viewpoint, good is respect for human personality. Evil is disregard for personality."

In seeking to make the eternal choice between good and

bad, there are those who would say, "Let your conscience be your guide." This strange spark of the divine within us cannot be disregarded nor should it be extinguished. But to be a sure guide, one's conscience must be enlightened and educated. It must go beyond a concern merely for one's self to a concern for others. What is not good for me is not good for others. The good increases welfare for others. Bad is that which weakens or destroys our fellows.

Our decisions of what is good and bad should come up out of our experience of life. Only, it must not be merely our own personal experience, but also that of others as we evaluate these as recorded in human history—and the Bible is one of the most helpful of these records. There are those who are willing to take the Bible as their sole guide. However, no one, regardless of his theory of the Bible, can escape an evaluation of the moral standards of those parts of the Bible, particularly the Old Testament which complacently accepts child-sacrifice, polygamy and the savagery of war.

Nevertheless, we should study the Bible. It is the record of mankind's quest to know God, and we should nurture our religious life. These two things are paramount in the discerning of good and evil. In God is life. We must seek to know Him and His spirit. We can come to know God through the life and spirit of Jesus. As we are motivated by the spirit of God, as revealed by Jesus, we come to understand God and to know what He requires. As we harmonize our life with the Creative Spirit, we can discern good from evil.

Thus, in determining whether a thing is good or bad, right or wrong, we would do well to seek to determine what the enlightened conscience has to say; what is the prompting of the "still, small voice within?" We should seek out the experience of history, especially the noble ethics of the Scripture, and particularly the New Testament. In these we can come to an understanding of the will and way of the eternal God in whose creativity we have life.

Having followed these two approaches seriously, a further help may bring certainty. We can apply the test of universality. Suppose our personal decision should become universal custom. Would it bring the world happiness or unhappiness, weal or woe, good or bad? Does it stand the test of time?

The difference between good and bad, right and wrong stands for all generations just where it stood when the Ten Commandments were formulated, or the Sermon on the Mount spoken. And for us in this dynamic age, the judgment must be based upon the living, contemporary reality written in the facts all about us. Truth, integrity, justice, equity, mercy, meekness, good will, peace, love—these are good and true and right, not just because somebody said so, but because history and the universe say so. God says so!

In our way of life we must cultivate a consciousness of the difference of good and bad, right and wrong which will well up within us as creatures of the Power in which we live. Whatever is good and right and true is rooted in the eternal order, and it cannot be uprooted. What is evil contributes to its own destruction. What is good is eternal. God is eternal.

2. THE MEASURE OF GREATNESS

Jesus said, "Whoever would be great among you must be the servant of all. For he that is least among you the same is great." Jesus' standard of greatness is as revolutionary as anything in his religion. In his day, as all too often in our day, the great were considered to be the men of wealth, authority and power, and the rulers of the land.

Right now, when we see the sorry spectacle of some men going about to convince people of their greatness and their future place in history, we need to consider the true qualities of greatness. It is not position, prestige or power. The greatness of a man is measured by his selflessness, his integrity and, above all, his humility. The contemporary estimate of greatness can often be wrong. History gives the ultimate estimate.

Again, Jesus taught: "Everyone that exaltest himself shall be humbled and everyone that humbles himself will be exalted." Humility is the real road to greatness. Tiberius Caesar would have been, according to an opinion poll in Jerusalem in Jesus' time (27 A.D.) acclaimed as the greatest living person.   And in Palestine, the greatest ones would have been Pilate and Herod and perhaps Caiaphas, the High Priest, persons who very name would have been lost from history had they not made themselves notorious by condemning the humble Galilean to the cross. Jesus was scarcely recognized as one of the great by the leaders and the historians of his time.

Josephus, the Jewish historian, living in Jerusalem 36-66 A.D., and dying in Rome 95 A.D., gave Jesus one short paragraph in his *Jewish Antiquities*. Later four other historians of that time gave passing mention of Jesus: Tacitus' *Annals*; Pliny's *Epistles*; Suetonius' *Lives of the Twelve Caesars*; and the Jewish Talmud. But since that time, historians have written volumes about Jesus.

> Speak history, who are life's victors?
> Unroll thy long annals and say.
> Are they whom the world calls victors,
> Who won the success of a day?
>
> The martyrs or Nero? The Spartans
> Who fell at Thermopylea's trist,
> Or the Persians or Xerxes? His judges
> Or Socrates? Pilate or Christ?
> —*N. W. Story*

It took the vision of a seer to discern that the truly great man of that first century A.D. was the Galilean martyr, Jesus. Some thirty years after that martyrdom, Paul of Tarsus wrote: "Wherefore God also highly exalted him, and gave him a name which is above every name; that in the name of Jesus every knee should bow . . . and that every tongue confess that Jesus Christ is Lord, to the glory of God." (Phil. 2:9-11) The astonishing thing is that the verdict of history has stamped Paul's estimate of greatness as true. Though lacking every claim to greatness conferred by wealth, social standing and power, the name of Jesus stands today at the head of humanity's greatest.

It is not a man's birth or blood or possessions which make him great, but what he really is, and the spirit of humility and service shown in his life. It is the quality of one's life. "Everyone that exalteth himself shall be humbled; but he that humbles himself shall be exalted."

Humility is not an inferiority complex. Far from it; it is something beautiful. It is a consciousness of an inner power. Jesus was humble, but he had a sense of power. "I have overcome the world," he said. "I have power to lay down my life, I have power to take it up." "You call me Lord and Master, and you are right, for so I am." He was master because he was humble. "I can do nothing of myself," he said. It was with the spirit of God that he served.

Jesus went further in expressing his idea of greatness when he used the illustration of the little child. "He called to him a little child and sat him in the midst of them, and said, 'Verily I say unto you, except you turn and become as little children, you shall in no wise enter the kingdom of heaven. Whoever, therefore, shall humble himself as this little child, the same is great in the kingdom of heaven.'" (Matt. 18:2-5)

So, his final word on greatness brings us to the spiritual

might of childlikeness. Greatness is the humility, the winsomeness, the purity of the child. Herein lies life.

Beyond this Jesus has little to say about greatness, but he demonstrated it in the heroic climax of his life. On the cross his final note of greatness is sacrifice. Here is supreme greatness. The world's great have always been those who have been willing to give themselves in some worthy cause.

Jesus' greatness lay in the fact that he gave himself in order to challenge men with the fact and love of the living God.

3. TURNING LIFE'S DEFEATS INTO VICTORIES

A prominent and successful man, upon his retirement, said to a group of friends, "The one thing I always wanted to do, I have not been granted." How often this has been repeated by others. How many people there are who have been unable to do what they wanted most to do. All around us are men and women living at their second choice. Phillips Brooks wanted to be a teacher, but he became a preacher—and what a preacher! Whistler wanted to go to West Point and become a military man; he became a painter. How many have had to live at their second best! I went to the university to do my graduate work and study social forces, economics and city problems hoping to serve in the ghettos and slums of the city; but most of my ministry has been in college and university pastorates. Life is a dark highway. The way ahead is often dim and unpredictable. Many have had to change course. Many have failed.

As with individuals, so with nations. America set out with the patriot's dream that sees beyond the years: an "America, the beautiful." Where are those high visions? America is going through one of those periods of the second best. Crises, struggles for power and profits, spiraling living costs, credibility gaps, and questionable integrity in high places in government.

What has religion to say to the defeated? What has religion to say to individuals and nations living at their second best?

The first thing that religion has to say is, *"Face it."* Face it intelligently. Do not panic. Defeat may even be a blessing in disguise. Jesus one time said, "Blessed are you when men shall revile you and persecute you...." Let us always look at the causes of failure or defeat. If the cause is of ourself, let us make every effort to amend. We are not always responsible for the failures which come to us. Often they come through no remedial fault of our own. Jesus is no failure, yet it was once recorded of him, "He could do no mighty work there." Why? It was because of the little faith of the people. I once knew a highly successful minister, who went to serve a church. He failed in three years, not because of his own abilities but because of the attitude of the congregation. Failure must be faced realistically.

The second thing religion has to say about our failures is: *"Use it."* Jesus used his seeming defeats. "We have always had a curious feeling that though we crucified Christ on a stick, he somehow managed to get hold of the right end of it, and that, if we were better men, we might try his plan," so wrote George Bernard Shaw. How true. If defeat comes to us, let us use it. We may not always be responsible for our failures and defeats, but we are responsible for the way we use them.

Our trials may be transmuted into triumphs. "Mill stones may become stepping stones." Religion can transform weights into wings. Our defeats and failures may become the refining tools of our character. We must take a positive attitude. We cannot do just nothing. If we do, we can become embittered. It is difficult to be defeated, but it is terrible to surrender to defeat. Multitudes use their defeats. They take up arms "against a sea of trouble." Sir Walter Scott did not let his blindness or his debts defeat him. Rather his deep character was revealed then more than in his days of achievement. Franklin Roosevelt surged on in spite of his paralysis. "Our greatest glory consists not in never falling but in rising every time we fall."

Again, when failure and defeat come, religion says, *"Glory in it."* Robert Browning wrote, "So may a glory from defeat arise." The cross, the symbol of defeat and shame, became the symbol of triumph. Now the Church sings, "In the Cross of Christ I glory." Paul who suffered much wrote, "In all things we are more than conquerors through Christ."

Let it not be implied that one should go about courting martyrdom, but there are some things worse than defeat. For the leader of the people to lose the confidence of the people, to lose his integrity—this is worse than defeat. When William Lloyd Garrison was defeated and maligned by the mobs in Boston for his stand on slavery, he could say: "We may be personally defeated, but our principles never." Truth and right ultimately prevail.

When Victor Hugo's Jean Val Jean had rightfully risen to a place of esteem, he learned that a simple, ignorant man was to be condemned for life because he was judged to be Jean Val Jean. So Jean Val Jean went and declared himself, revealing his identity. It was a noble thing to do. In doing so he held to his integrity. In such nobility of character, rising out of integrity, lies the mystery of greatness. As Jesus put it, "What will it profit a man if he gain the whole world and lose his soul."

It is not whether we have won or lost,
It's how we've played the game.

4. GOOD MEN WHO HAVE FAILED

If you are good you will succeed is a statement which must be questioned. It must be questioned because goodness must be held above price. Many good men have failed.

This idea of goodness bringing success comes up out of an old Hebrew concept. Whenever the ancient Hebrews succeeded, regardless of how evil were their motives, it was their goodness which had brought victory. Whenever disaster overtook them, regardless of how innocent they were, it was because they had sinned or because they had an Achan in their camp. But this ancient concept does not hold true.

The more worthy concept is "good for goodness sake," not good for the rewards or success it brings. "Seek first the kingdom of God and his uprightness and all else shall be yours." This is seen in its real significance in Luke 18: 29-30 when Jesus assured his disciples that those who gave up everything for the kingdom of God "will receive manifold more in this time, and in the age to come eternal life." They did give their all to God. They suffered martyrdom. They failed, but they changed the course of human history.

Many early Christians suffered martyrdom. We have more respect for them than for some of the early Christian Emperors. The former were true to their Christianity, while the latter at times betrayed it.

Let us look at a few of the good men who have failed. Jeremiah, the weeping prophet, loved his God. He was a real patriot, but he condemned his nation's sins and sinners. A wicked king persecuted him and had him thrown into a pit. Savonarola, a saint, uncanonized, persecuted, tortured, excommunicated, gave his all for Florence, in the end burned at the stake. John Hus, Rector of the University of Prague, who, because of his leadership in religious reform, was dismissed, degraded and burned at the stake. William Tyndale, brilliant Oxford scholar, translated the New Testament and part of the Old Testament into English, was hunted down and later burned at the stake. Jonathan Edwards, a brilliant and fearless servant of the Church, was forced to resign and banished from the colony. These and a glorious host of others, up through the centuries, were good men who failed.

All this is not to say that all good men fail; quite the contrary.   St. Augustine succeeded while Rome fell. St. Francis of Assisi, John Knox, John Wesley, Thomas Jefferson, Gandhi, Jane Addams, Kagawa and Schweitzer, to name but a few; all were successful.   Nor, let it be remembered, do all wicked men succeed; their failures are legion.

The success or failure of men must be viewed in the perspective of history rather than by their contemporaries. Many, in his lifetime, thought that Lincoln was a failure, but history proved them wrong. Woodrow Wilson failed with his League of Nations, but he laid the foundation for world government.   John the Baptist failed.   His was a voice crying in the wilderness.   He lost his head; but, he was the great forerunner of the Christ.

Jesus of Nazareth, the best man who ever lived, failed. No man ever claimed so much and realized so little in his lifetime. He had followers—multitudes; but when the test came, even his intimate disciples deserted him. He preached "The kingdom of God is at hand."   But, instead of a coronation, a crucifixion was his earthly end; instead of praise, he received curses; instead of a throne, he bore a cross.   To multitudes of his day he was a failure, but today he towers above all other personalities.   Great art, great literature, great institutions have been created in his name. Even time is measured by his birth.   He changed human history.   We call him the Rock of Ages because he stands in the midst of the storms of time and eternity. Even Ernest Renan, the French skeptic, thinking of Jesus, wrote: "Thou art destined to become the cornerstone of humanity in such wise that to tear thy name from this world would be to shake it to its foundations."

In the final analysis, in the perspective of history, in the test of time, the good men never fail.

It is only time and God can judge.

> Great men have lived
> In ages gone; with power they ruled the world.
> But time is fleet; their banners now are furled,
> And who today is grieved?

> Now, other men
> Have climbed to fame; how proud and sure their power.
> But they—how soon—will spend their little hour
> And be obscured again.

> Apart from fame,
> There lived a man to whom mere power was dross
> He did God's will—and died upon a cross—
> And earth reveres his name.
> —*Thomas Curtis Clark*

5. WHERE THERE IS NO DEFEAT

For the just, the upright, the person of integrity, there is no defeat. God has a way of giving power to the defeated and of transforming failure into victory. "The stone which the builders rejected became the head of the corner."

"The blood of the martyrs became the seed of the Church." When Joseph appeared before his brothers, who had sold him as a slave into Egypt, he said to them, "What you meant as evil against me God turned it into good." This is the nature and way of God. It is the process of the cosmic order: healing where there is hurt and righting where there is wrong.

This is the message that our world needs today, a message of triumph over defeat. We have been urged to think about what is right about our country and our world; but we cannot stick our heads into the sand, ostrich-like, and ignore what is wrong. Nations are struggling to keep from annihilating each other. People are confused and baffled. Crime has become a terror in our cities and countryside. Morals are dissipated. All about us is a lack of integrity and failing confidence. Our souls are so filled with confusion and fear that we fail to hear the words of the world's great leader: "In the world you will have trouble, but take courage. I have conquered the world." He could say this because later in Gethsemane he could say to God, "Thy will be done."

Who can separate us from the love of God, shall tribulation or corruption or exploitation or nuclear destruction or lack of confidence or moral disorder? No, "in all these things we are more than conquerors through him who loved us." We should be sure that neither life, nor death, nor cover-ups, nor powerful interests, nor present moral disorder, nor more revelations yet to come, nor powers high and low, nor anything else in our confused world will be able to separate us from the love of God. Without God we are defeated; with God there is no defeat.

We need a new prophet like Amos to focus the attention of the nation on the fundamental needs for moral justice and ethical integrity in every phase of our life, and who will cause "justice (to) roll down like waters." We desperately need God-fearing leaders like Abraham Lincoln, who, when faced with a critical situation and asked to change his decision, replied, "I would rather die than change." And on an earlier occasion, when Lincoln was a member of the Illinois legislature, he said, "You may burn my body to ashes and scatter them to the winds of heaven. You may drop my soul down to the regions of darkness and despair to be tormented forever, but you will never get me to support a measure which I believe to be wrong."

The contemporary crisis in morality and government has forced upon us the irony of our present situation in which man, after the long march up the ages, can all but reach out and grasp humanity's true destiny, finds himself bogged down in moral confusion. The cruel fact is that a civilization which possesses the technology, the capacity and the intelligence should lack the courage and the character to achieve full greatness; that a civilization, which possesses the knowledge of universal laws to send men out into space and land them on the moon, has not yet acquired the truth which sets men free.

We do not know what the future holds, but we should know that what happens to this planet tomorrow turns upon man's complete harmony with the earth, the home of his soul, and with his harmony with his creator—God.

If the long reach of history has anything to teach us it is that there is no defeat for truth. "Truth crushed to earth will rise again." Right will not be forever on the scaffold. There is an eternal sense of justice at the heart of this orderly universe. Sooner or later the just cause wins; the righteous person triumphs. Even the stars in their courses are moving in orderliness. The whole cosmic order is striving for harmony and right.

There is no defeat for God. Only nations, empires and civilizations are defeated and crumble away when they forget God and ignore the laws of His universe. His laws cannot be broken; only men are broken when they forget or ignore them. God is eternal, and the people who recognize the Power in which they live and move and have their being shall live.

Let the discouraged take courage for back of them is truth. Let the defeated in a just cause take hope for back of them is the cosmic order. Let the righteous keep faith for back of them is the eternal God.

SECTION XXI

THE UNIVERSE

XXI. THE UNIVERSE

1. The Environment of the Soul
2. Standing on the Edge of Mystery

1. THE ENVIRONMENT OF THE SOUL

As our civilization enters into the closing years of this dynamic twentieth century, grave environmental problems lie ahead. The solution of these will have much to do in the determining of human destiny.

The most startling discovery of this fast-moving space age is that our planet is not indestructible, nor are its resources limitless. The energy crisis is only one of the anxious concerns of serious-minded leaders. Concern for the physical condition of our earth weighs heavily upon thoughtful people. A catastrophic end of the earth is now not only the erratic fantasy of a few fanatical religionists, but a possible reality which forces itself upon human intelligence.

For some time now, intelligent people have known that ascending life on this planet is possible only because unnumbered millions of factors are regulated and motivated in precise balance under cosmic laws. Never before, as in our rapidly expanding twentieth century, has the ecological balance been so threatened. Life is now imperiled not because of any failure of cosmic design, but because of human failure, ignorance and selfishness.

We are living in a universe. Our earth is a part of that universe, a most beautiful even though a very small part.

Where in all this universe could there be found a more wonderfully beautiful place in which to live? The earth, with its towering mountains, its restless seas, its green valleys, its beautiful trees, shrubs and flowers, its delicious fruits and all things to sustain life, is the wonderful, creative home of the soul of man.

Have you ever paused to consider how fortunate you are to have had the privilege of living upon this beautiful planet at this moment of cosmic history? We are one with the whole cosmic order. We must seek to learn and to understand more of the cosmic laws in order that all life—yours and mine and all that come after us—may have fuller life.

Too long have we lived in thoughtless, even indifferent carelessness in our use of the earth and its environment. We have prodigally used the fertility of the soil, its fresh flowing waterways, its natural resources and energy. We have carelessly polluted the atmosphere. Smog hovers over our cities. Atomic fall-out, atomic waste, chemicals which cause disease, water pollution—these and other problems indicate that an emergency is already confronting us. These present a challenge to contemporary scientists and technicians.

Greater human intelligence must be developed in order to maintain a proper balance between resources and need, to retain the natural environment in order to keep pure air to breathe and water to drink, to balance our whole ecology in order to assure a wholesome atmosphere in which humanity can live and progress.

Here is a task for the dedicated scientist and technician to point the way. But more, a concerted, consecrated effort is needed on the part of all dedicated people to work with the Power back of the universe in which we live.

In the final analysis, mankind must harmonize with the universe of which he is a part, with the Power back of the universe. Only working with God can we live safely, abundantly and happily on this terrestrial sphere.

"The earth is the Lord's and the fulness thereof, the world and those who dwell therein"; the soul of the earth is man and the love of man.

2. STANDING ON THE EDGE OF MYSTERY

We stand on the edge of mystery. "The heavens declare the glory of God. The firmament showeth his handiwork." The mysteries of this vast universe lure man's adventurous spirit on, they challenge his creativeness, they enhance his soul. He strives to know the unknowable.

The quest for knowledge and understanding in this dynamic age goes increasingly on. Man, by his creative spirit and his inventive genius, moves out into space, eager to learn what lies beyond his earth. He has walked on the moon. He has made fantastic pictures of the planet Mars. The mystery of the moon, the planets and the stars lures us on with the hope that the limited can comprehend the limitless, and the finite fathom the infinite. As yet "we see in a mirror dimly." We stand on the edge of mystery!

The vastness of our universe staggers our imagination. The range of man's vision in the universe is limited to the nearest stars. The range of his mind goes farther. Astronomers have tried to help us to comprehend the vastness. They tell us that the nearest star to our earth, Alpha Centauri, is 25,000,000,000,000 miles away, or 4.3 light years away, which is to say, it takes light from the nearest star, traveling 186,000 miles per second 4.3 years to reach our earth. The farthest point of light in the heavens, which is visible to the unaided eye, is a nebula some 900,000 light years away. Through powerful radio telescopes, the light of other stars can be seen.

How vast, how mysterious our universe is! It staggers
our imagination!   Beyond our solar system are other
galaxies of systems.   Out into space are other myriads of
galaxies. Space seems limitless. Where does it end? Where
does it begin? Is space limitless and time timeless? Though
the range of the human mind seems infinite, the universe
is beyond our comprehension.

Vast though the universe is, to the astronomer the great
impressive marvel is not the vastness, but the orderliness of
the universe.   Everything moves in precise orderliness.
There is nothing haphazard, everything is in precision; no
chaos, only cosmos.

As I have gazed up into the starry heavens, I, as you,
have been filled with wonder and awe, such as to leave
one's soul filled with wonder and worship of something
greater beyond.   In years past, on balmy summer evenings,
I have lain prone with my children looking up at the stars
above, and heard my children ask, "What are the stars?"
How I, too, have wondered what they are! Somehow, my
thoughts turned to God.

"O God, how great Thou art!"

"How excellent is thy name in all the earth." Only God
can "bind the chains of the Pleiades, and loose the cords of
Orion." We hold with Emerson that "Nature is too thin a
screen; the glory of the omnipresent God bursts through
everywhere." The mystery of the universe and the orderliness of the cosmic order are shrouded in unfathomable
obscurity until we learn that all laws suppose a law-giver,
and that all creation involves a creator. Surely,

> "The heavens declare the glory of God
>   and the firmament proclaims his handiwork."

What is it all about? Wherein lies the meaning of the
universe?   The answer lies not in the experience which
comes through the eye, whether of the vast infinity of
the starry heavens, even though aided with powerful

radio telescopes, nor in the amazing world of the atom revealed by high-power microscopes. The experience must lie deeper in that which is timeless and eternal. The vastness of space and the cosmic orderliness all point to a purposeful creation, to the truth that there is an intelligent purpose back of it all.

The knowledge of this mysterious universe must be sought in reason, meaning and purpose. The great creative Power from which all cosmic life emerges has not brought humanity up through the long processes of the centuries for some idle purpose. In the final analysis, the mystery of the universe will be revealed through man working creatively with the Power in which he lives and moves and has his being—God. God is spirit. Only the spiritual transcends all time and eternity.

Standing on the edge of mystery, it does not yet appear what we shall be; but we know that "when he appears we shall be like him." We have faith in the future of humanity because we have faith in the universe and its creative God. The mystery of it all challenges the questing spirit of man: "Climb higher and higher; Sail on, sail on; Jet into orbit after orbit." "Quest farther and farther into the yet unknown."

Standing on the edge of mystery we try to grasp it with our finite mind. "You shall know the truth." said Jesus, "and the truth will make you free."

SECTION XXII

WORSHIP

XXII. WORSHIP

1. The Worship of God

1. THE WORSHIP OF GOD

"The most important thing in the life of a nation is the worship of God in Church on Sunday."

"A congregation devoutly engaged in worship is doing something for a community that can be done in no other way; it is sending up a collective witness to God," so wrote Charles Edward Jefferson, for many years the minister of Broadway Tabernacle, New York City. Worship can be meaningful. It becomes increasingly so when engaged in with sincerity.

There is a natural and logical sequence to the worship of God. While this holds true for individual worship, it is especially true for congregational worship. The ancient Hebrews seem to have learned this. One of the finest illustrations of this is to be found in the experience of Isaiah as recorded in Isaiah 6:1-8. Read it.

Isaiah, a young nobleman, who later became one of the great Hebrew prophets, felt sorely the great loss when the good King Uzziah died. Evidently, following the funeral of the King, Isaiah sat alone in the Temple in sorrowful meditation. The smoke rising from the dying embers upon the great altar gave imagery to his meditation. In these moments of *silent meditation*, Isaiah became *aware of God.* "I saw the Lord sitting upon a throne, high and lifted up," he rcorded. And he recalled the re-echoing anthem of the Temple Choir singing,

> "Holy, holy, holy is the Lord of hosts;
> the whole earth is full of his glory."

Through his quiet meditation Isaiah, becoming aware of God, is stirred with the greatness and majesty of God, and there wells up within him *Praise to God.*

Awed by the majesty and greatness of God, Isaiah becomes *aware of himself.* This awareness of himself brings a sense of humility, a need for recognition of his weakness, a *confession of sin and intercession* to God. In deep sincerity, Isaiah cried out, "Woe is me! For I am lost; for I am a man of unclean lips, and I dwell in the midst of a people of unclean lips." When in sincere humility Isaiah confesses his sin and the people's sin, he hears the assurance of forgiveness: "Your guilt is taken away, and your sin is forgiven." Here are moments of *confession, intercession and forgiveness.*

How transforming the assurance of forgiveness can be! Life takes on a greater assurance and a new courage. Life is open and ready for *spiritual illumination.* Thus, Isaiah says: "Mine eyes have seen the Lord." "I heard the voice of the Lord saying, 'Whom shall I send, and who will go for us?'" In silent meditation Isaiah, through an awareness of God and his own sinful self, and humbly confessing his sin and sensing forgiveness, now is ready for a challenge from God. (The voice could be God's or a minister of the Lord through challenging preaching.) This is the sequence through which worship transmutes itself into life. Just as "faith without works is dead," so worship without action is futile. Worship is not an end in itself; it fulfills itself in the pursuit of the abundant life.

Isaiah meets the challenge: "Here I am! Send me." This is the ultimate goal of worship. This is the true value of worship: *the dedication of life*. "Send me!" Use my hands, my feet, my voice, my brain to fulfill Thy purpose, Thy truth, Thy love. And the Lord said, "Go and speak to the people."

Here is the logical sequence of worship:
Personal Meditation
Praise to God
Confession, Intercession and Forgiveness
Spiritual Illumination
The Dedication of Life (symbolized by the offering)
The Benediction

The benediction. As in the beginning, so at the close of worship, let there be silence. The minister and congregation should have these closing moments in silence before God to say "Here I am! Send me!"—each in a personal dedication. The organ postlude comes like the echoing voice of God; the chimes like the vibrations of infinite peace.

SECTION XXIII

CONCLUSION

XXIII. CONCLUSION

1. What an Age!
2. The Challenge of Crisis
3. What of the Future?

1. WHAT AN AGE!

What an age in which to live! Progress in the past few decades has been nothing less than marvelous. It was undreamed of a couple of generations ago. Man's ability to produce food without the arduous toil of bygone days, innumerable gadgets to do chores and drudgery, comforts of homes and places to work, resources of energy to serve—if they are not dissipated—motor cars, airplanes to give wings to travel, instant communication around the globe, men walking on the moon! What an age!

The technological revolution taking place in our generation is capable of producing such an increasing abundance that no one anywhere need ever know want again. Thinking in terms of the material, the achievements of human intelligence have literally projected us into an age of abundance where all human life could be enhanced by this resource-full earth.

Yet, with the awesome creativeness of man's intellect; with the greatest economic prosperity ever known; with scientific accomplishments unparalled in human history; and with a technology whose machines and methods continually computerize and revolutionize our way of life; with all this, we are neglecting the very heart and soul of our culture, and are standing in serious danger of losing it. By our selfishness, our self-seeking, our greed, our lust for power, and our lack of wisdom we are denying ourselves the beneficent resources of our planet.

We are a nation of activists, problem-solvers, inventors and would-be maker of gadgets. Our prevailing concern has been the conquest of nature, the production of material goods, and the development of political government. The emphasis of recent years has been the development of energy and power, nuclear fission and the exploration of space.

While we have been doing this we have been forgetting man, his social, moral, ethical and spiritual life. We have been neglecting the deeper concerns of men today and the days yet to be. Too often as a nation and as individuals we have shifted the emphasis of our living from building the inner resources to gaining outward success. This has brought many difficulties—wars, depletion of resources, inflation. Our dynamic generation feels driven and spiritually exhausted. In our age of material things, we measure success by the number of things we possess. Our standards of success are entangled with the desire for acquisition.

Not that success is unworthy or undesirable. Quite the opposite. Any success that is well and wisely achieved is an excellent thing, calling for courage and discipline and diligence. The thing to be avoided, the thing against which Jesus continually warned, is mere material success which is achieved at the expense of spiritual growth, and the development of character and personality. "What shall it profit a man though he gain the whole world and lose his own soul." In the story which Jesus told of the rich man and his barns, you will recall that God condemned the man as a fool, not because he was rich, not because he had become successful, but because, in the process of becoming rich and successful, he had neglected his soul.

God, through His marvelous creativity, has given us a world of unlimited resources of power. He has blessed us and enhanced the life of man with an abundance to meet every need. Wherever there is want, it is the result of man's greed and lust for possessions and power. The physical and material environment is essential to man's physical life; but we must come to realize fully that, if mankind is to achieve full humanity, man cannot live by bread alone, but by the spirit and the way of the Creator—God.

The American people are capable of dedication and greatness. A great movement and hope could sweep across America and the world if, somehow, we could rededicate ourselves and find a national leader and a Congress which would listen to the aspirations of the people, and who would respond with leadership in the commitment of America's creativity and power to lead America and the world into a "race" not for armaments, but a movement to use the resources and the energy of the earth for the welfare, the health, the development of all the people on this terrestrial sphere.

Do not say this cannot be done. It ought, it can, it must be done if humanity is to fulfill its worthy destiny.

This is a challenge equal to this dynamic age. A few years ago a young President challenged America to place a man on the Moon within a decade. Even some scientists said it could not be done. But within the decade, men walked on the Moon. How worthy, how wonderful it could be for America to lead the world in lasting peace, security and the abundant life for all as effectively as "the arsenal for democracy" led in the development of weaponry.

"In the world you will have trouble," said Jesus, "but take courage, I have conquered the world." Victory will come to all who follow in His way.

What an age in which to live!
To be alive in such an age!
With every year a lightning page
Turned in the world's great wonder-book
Whereon the leaning nations look,
Where men speak strong of brotherhood,
For peace and universal good,
When miracles are everywhere,
And every inch of common air
Throbs a tremendous prophecy
Of greater marvels yet to be.
O, Thrilling Age!
O, Willing Age!
When steel and stone and rail and rod
Welcome the utterance of God—
A trumpet to shout his wonder through
Proclaiming all that man can do.

To be alive in such an age!
To live in it!
To give in it!

* * * * *

Give thanks with all thy flaming heart,
Crave but to have in it a part—
Give thanks and grasp thy heritage—
To be alive in such an age!
                                —*Angela Morgan*

2. THE CHALLENGE OF CRISIS

We are facing the day in human history which thinking
men approach with awe and wonder—the day when man

would become all-powerful, when no one could defeat or destroy without being defeated or destroyed, or, on the other hand, triumph without the triumph of all. We are not sure that we have the wisdom and the stamina to survive. "These are times that try men souls," although spoken of an earlier age, more aptly apply to our own.

We have been bombarded on all sides today by the cry of crisis, crisis. The cry of crisis has become a weariness to the brain. Almost everywhere we turn we are confronted with the cry of crisis: there is crisis in energy, crisis in economy, crisis in government. Also, there is crisis in the Middle East and crisis in Africa. Yet, every age is critical and fraught with destiny. However, in the wide survey of history, ours seems to be most crucial in shaping the destiny of man on this planet.

Scarcity of any vital necessity during peacetime is a new and jolting experience to the American people who have had the highest standard of living of any people on earth. In this prosperous nation, on this rich continent, it should never have happened. Careful researchers and scientists assure us that America can ride through any crisis provided that selfish, private interests do not continue to have priority over public need.

The technological revolution taking place in our generation is capable of producing such an abundance that no person anywhere need ever know scarcity and insecurity again. When we have gained the wisdom and the intelligence to stop the drain of the creative skills and manpower, and of the precious resources of the earth, caused by the stupidity of war, the bright hopes and dreams of man could become the reality, and abundant life come for all.

The awesomeness of man's intellect has already projected us into a new era, but the end is not yet. Greater possibilities lie ahead. Man's intellect is equal to the opportunities, for out of the unfathomable range of his mind, before which the scientists stand awed, man has shown the capacity to realize his dreams.

Yet, by the greatest prosperity as yet known by man; with scientific accomplishments unparalleled in human history; and with a technology whose machines and methods continually computerize and revolutionize our way of life, we are neglecting and standing in serious danger of losing much of the hard-won gains of the past.

The entrance into a beneficent future depends upon man's achievements in the spiritual realm. Man has largely mastered the material realm, its machines and its scientific technology. But there are still more difficult barriers to be broken down: selfishness, greed, lust for power, prejudice, hatred, and brutal violence. When man has been able to remove these barriers, he will begin to see the end of destructive racial disorders and wars—all things which have faced a nation of people with crises—and, at long last, will advance near to the realization of the way of life embodied in our Judeo-Christian heritage.

The right use of the physical environment and the material resources are essential to man's physical life; but we must come to the realization that, if man is to live in prosperity, security and peace on this terrestrial sphere, he cannot live by bread alone, but by the way and the spirit of Him in whom he has life and very being—God.

3. WHAT OF THE FUTURE?

What of the future? What is the future of America? We are now well launched into the third century of America as a nation of people. What will this third century bring as America is thrust into the future?

The first century of America was a period of worthy, sacrificial and heroic effort to build strong the foundations of the new nation founded on liberty, freedom and justice, and to forge the bonds which would bind a sprawling nation into a unity. Sturdy men went out and "a thorough-fare for freedom beat across the wilderness." Out of the wilderness they hewed homes and developed farms and towns and cities. Those were the "horse and buggy days," when men toiled hard on farms and in factories. They were also the days of cruel and regretful times, testing whether a nation "so conceived and so dedicated could long endure." It endured.

With unity preserved, and with dedication, the nation entered its second century. And what a century! The achievements in material progress and wealth have been almost unbelievable. It was a period of physical and material growth unequalled by any other century. The "Horseless carriage" became the automobile which has transformed the lifestyle of the people. It produced the radio and television, the airplane which now travels with the speed of sound, automation, space exploration, men going to and from the moon, and America now the leader to whom all nations look for direction.

Now, what of Third Century America? The possibilities seem to be limitless: space shuttle, solar energy, conquered diseases, etc.—material progress yet undreamed! If—

Truly, materially, scientifically and technologically man's achievements have been marvelous, undreamed of a century ago. But what of man himself? What about the social, ethical, moral and spiritual development of mankind?

The real goal of mankind is not merely material, nor the development of the latent powers of the human mind with which man has been endowed by his Creator, but also the cultivation of man's soul. What is happening to man's soul, his social relations, his ethics, his spirit? This determines human progress and destiny. In the final analysis, the measure of mankind's progress is not how fast or how far he can travel on this planet or out into space, it is how well he can live on this terrestrial sphere in security and peace.

What is the present—the realistic picture? Crime in the streets, murder, rape, violence in movies and on TV, cheating, lack of morals and integrity in high places, building big debts and declaring bankruptcy, drunkenness, causing carnage on the highways, drug addiction, unions demanding higher wages, corporations demanding bigger profits, professionals ready to strike for higher salary, spiraling living-costs. Every sizeable city is building ever larger arenas and stadiums for physical combat but with no money for art and temples of worship. The government spends increasing billions for weapons for human destruction—all of this portrays a very unpromising trend in American life.

Will this trend increase and eventually destroy human progress? Will it gain ascendency over the dedicated scientist seeking to isolate diseases, or the ecologist striving to preserve earth's environment, or the selfless men and women who are truly concerned about what happens to their fellow beings and who are striving to bring the abundant life to all regardless of race, nation, creed or class?

What Edward Gibbons wrote about ancient Greece is wholly relevant to America now: when the Athenians came to want security and comfort more than responsibility, when they wanted more from society than they were willing to give to it, "then Athens ceased to be free." He further pointed out that Rome fell not so much because of the enemies without, but because of the decadent, immoral life of its citizens.

Truly, there are signs of moral progress. There are many selfless, dedicated people striving courageously to cultivate the human spirit. There are multitudes who are giving conscious effort to seek the better finer, higher moral and spiritual life.

But, aside from the thrust of our computerized atomic weapons, are we much further advanced than the Athenians or the Romans under the Caesars? We are still grappling with the same human problems of character. There is a difference: we have history. Will we learn from it?

Would that this beginning of a Third Century America become a watershed, and that we, the people, would turn away from the things that degrade this fair land; and would that we commit ourselves to the responsibilities essential to achieving the dream of America, the beautiful; would that we might ask with a young American President: "Ask not what your country can do for you, but what you can do for your country."

The range of the human mind is infinite, and the potentialities of the human spirit are immortal. The dream of the ages is before us. The quest is ours. The quality of life in this Third Century America, and the whole world, is beyond our fondest dreams if each of us would resolve to live the way of the Power which has given us breath and life and being, and this universe, our home. We dare not fumble the future. It is up to us.